TWAYNE'S ENGLISH AUTHORS SERIES

EDITOR OF THIS VOLUME

Bertram H. Davis

Florida State University

Thomas Southerne

TEAS 315

Thomas Southerne Esq.r

THOMAS SOUTHERNE

By ROBERT L. ROOT, JR.

Central Michigan University

TWAYNE PUBLISHERS

A DIVISION OF G. K. HALL & CO., BOSTON

Published in 1981 by Twayne Publishers,
A Division of G. K. Hall & Co.
All Rights Reserved

Printed on permanent/durable acid-free paper and bound
in the United States of America

First Printing

Library of Congress Cataloging in Publication Data

Root, Robert L.
Thomas Southerne.

(Twayne's English authors series; TEAS 315)
Bibliography: p. 143 - 48
Includes index.
1. Southerne, Thomas, 1660 - 1746—Criticism and
interpretation.
PR3699.S3Z8   822'.5   80-19162
ISBN 0-8057-6727-4

For my son, Thomas,
—of course

Contents

About the Author

Robert Root received the B.A. degree from State University College at Geneseo, New York, and the M.A. and Ph.D. degrees from the University of Iowa. His dissertation, "The Problematics of Marriage: English Comedy 1688 - 1710," focused chiefly on such figures as Southerne, Vanbrugh, Congreve, and Farquhar. He has published an article, "Aphra Behn, Arranged Marriage, and Restoration Comedy," in *Women & Literature*, a bibliography of Restoration studies in *Restoration*, and other notes and reviews in *PMLA*, *Notes & Queries*, and *Philological Quarterly*.

Professor Root teaches at Central Michigan University, where he is currently Director of Composition. He has spoken on composition theory and pedagogy and popular culture at meetings of the National Council of Teachers of English, the Conference on College Composition and Communication, the Canadian Council of Teachers of English, the Michigan Council of Teachers of English, and the Popular Culture Association. Two of those talks have been included in the ERIC system; one has been published in *Reinventing the Rhetorical Tradition*. He is also an officer of MCTE.

Professor Root received a Faculty Research and Creative Endeavors grant from Central Michigan University for research and travel on this TEAS Study of Thomas Southerne. He is currently writing and teaching a variety of writing courses at Central Michigan University.

Preface

In the past thirty years Thomas Southerne's reputation has grown considerably. Since John Harrington Smith expressed his regard for *The Wives Excuse* as "one of the five most considerable comedies written between 1660 and 1700," interest in Southerne's plays has increased, leading to his inclusion among the primary figures of the period in new surveys of Restoration drama, and to the publication and preparation of editions not only of individual plays but of the collected works as well. Thus the time has surely come for a thorough reappraisal of his accomplishments and of his place in Restoration drama.

I offer that reappraisal here. In doing so, I have been concerned to show the background of comic conventions in the Restoration, against which the unique qualities of Southerne's major comedies can be more sharply discerned, and the background of Restoration serious drama, to which his major tragedies were notable contributions. Thus my emphasis in the opening chapter has been on those aspects of Restoration drama which relate most to Southerne's work and to a just and accurate evaluation of his position in that drama. In each of the succeeding chapters—on his earliest plays, on each of his five most important plays, on his final productions, and on his accomplishments and critical reputation—I have been concerned to show the influences upon each play, the extent to which Southerne departed from norms and convention, and the characteristic elements of his work as they emerge, develop, and are modified throughout his career.

Finally, throughout, but especially in the opening and closing chapters, I have attempted to give some sense of the importance of Southerne and his drama to his time and to the drama of the eighteenth century. This has been no easy task: influences and significance are often hard to gauge and Southerne's impact, while hardly as negligible as it once was treated, is not as obviously measurable as it is with his better-known contemporaries. The degree to which Southerne embodied certain elements of the theater coalescing at the time does not necessarily reflect the degree to which he disseminated them. I have tried, nonetheless, to measure both as accurately as possible.

I have left much unsaid that I would like to say about Southerne's relationship to other writers, particularly to Congreve and Vanbrugh, and about Restoration drama in general, but much of it either is not immediately pertinent here or is inappropriate to the scope of this kind of study. Similarly, I have left largely unexamined some aspects of Southerne's biography, hoping to direct attention only to those events or relationships which have significance for his writing. In this restrained context, then, I will count the book successful if it helps the reader to recognize the richness and complexity of Southerne's work and leads him or her to speculate upon the significance of that work for English drama.

To complete this study I have placed myself in the debt of a good many people. Chiefly I must thank Carl H. Klaus, who first introduced me to Restoration drama and to Southerne, and Judith H. Milhous, who encouraged this study by contributing her advice to an early draft. My indebtedness extends as well to Ms. Helene E. Zeller of the Special Collections Room of the University of Iowa Library; to the staffs of the Newberry Library, the Folger Shakespeare Library, the University of Michigan Graduate Library, and Michigan State University Library; and to Joy Pastucha, Cecily Little, and the staff of the Park Library, Central Michigan Library, for their efforts on my behalf. I am grateful to Central Michigan University as well for partial funding of the research on this book. Special appreciation is reserved for my wife, Mary Kay, not only for reading copy, but for letting Thomas Southerne live with us so long.

ROBERT L. ROOT, JR.

Central Michigan University

Chronology

1659   Thomas Southerne, the son of Francis and Margaret Southerne, born on February 12 in the parish of St. Michan, Dublin. Early education at the grammar school of Edward Wetenhall.

1675   Enters Trinity College, Dublin University, as a pensioner on March 30.

1678   His father, a Dublin brewer, dies.

1680   Admitted to the Middle Temple, London, on July 15.

1682   *The Loyal Brother, or, The Persian Prince* performed by the King's Company at the Theatre Royal in Drury Lane in early February.

1684   *The Disappointment, or, The Mother in Fashion* produced by the United Company at the Theatre Royal in late March or early April.

1685   Enters the Princess Anne's Regiment in June with the rank of ensign and subsequently rises to the rank of captain.

1687   *The Spartan Dame* begun; abandoned because of unlikelihood of production.

1690   *Sir Anthony Love, or, The Rambling Lady*, Southerne's only popular comic success, produced at the Theatre Royal in late September or early October.

1691   *The Wives Excuse, or, Cuckolds Make Themselves* produced at the Theatre Royal in December.

1692   Assists Dryden in completing *Cleomenes, the Spartan Hero*. Assists Dryden and Mainwaring in preparing Congreve's *The Old Batchelor* for the stage.

1693   *The Maid's Last Prayer, or, Any Rather Than Fail* produced in March at the Theatre Royal. An epistle, "To Mr. Congreve," declaring him Dryden's heir, is published with *The Old Batchelor*.

1694   *The Fatal Marriage, or The Innocent Adultery* produced in February. Dryden ranks him with Etherege and Wycherley in an epistle to Congreve published with Congreve's *The Double Dealer*.

1695   *Oroonoko* produced by Rich's Company at the Theatre Royal in November. Helps Colley Cibber secure production of his play, *Love's Last Shift*.

1696   Writes the preface to Richard Norton's *Pausanias, The Betrayer of His Country*.

c.1696 -   Marries Agnes Atkyns, née Atkins, a widow with several
1700   children. She will predecease him.

1700   *The Fate of Capua* produced in April by Betterton's Company at Lincoln's Inn Fields; fails. Congreve's *The Way of the World* a moderate success. Both retire from the stage. Dryden dies May 1.

1704   Supports John Dennis's *Liberty Asserted,* a Whig play; seeks support from the Duke of Devonshire for *The Spartan Dame;* is lampooned in *The Tryal of Skill* for turning "Cat in Pan." He may also have become a regimental agent in the service of Charles Boyle, Earl of Orrery.

1713   Supervises the publication of *The Works of Thomas Southerne, Esq.,* including a preface and all eight previously published plays.

1714   Resigns as regimental agent.

1719   *The Spartan Dame* opens in early December at Drury Lane after the intercession of Congreve with the Duke of Newcastle wins it the right of performance. Pope's epigram "In Behalf of Mr. Southerne to the Duke of Argyle" is written about Argyle's response to Southerne's dedication of the play to him. Assists production of John Hughes's *The Siege of Damascus*.

1721   The second edition of the *Works,* including *The Spartan Dame*.

1723   In the dedication to *Mariamne* Elijah Fenton mentions Southerne's encouragement.

1726   *Money The Mistress,* his last play, fails upon production at Lincoln's Inn Fields February 19.

1729   Assists Samuel Madden in getting production of *Themistocles, The Lover of His Country*.

1733   Visits Swift in Dublin.

1736   Writes notes for a life of Congreve to appear in Thomas Birch's *General Dictionary, Historical and Critical,* never published.

1737   On Thursday, December 17, writes Dr. Richard Rawlinson to correct the entry in *Athenae Oxonienses* which claimed, among other errors, that he had been a servitor at Pembroke College, Oxford. He lists his ten plays in print and mentions his military service.

1742   Pope's poem "Tom Southerne's Birthday at Ld. Orrery's" is printed in the *Gentleman's Magazine* in February.

1745   Contributes the article "On the Poets and Actors in King Charles II's Reign" to the *Gentleman's Magazine* for February.

1746   Dies on May 26.

1764   His daughter, Agnes Egerton, dies.

1774   The third collection of his works is published as *Plays Written by Mr. Thomas Southerne, Esq.*, adding *Money the Mistress* and a biography by Thomas Evans.

CHAPTER 1

Thomas Southerne and the Restoration Stage

THOMAS Southerne's dramatic career involved him intimately with the leading playwrights of three different periods of English drama. From some he borrowed and learned, drawing from the Restoration stage milieu characters and themes to which he added his own special perspective. In his turn, Southerne contributed to the development of younger playwrights, advising them in their writing and assisting them in bringing their work to the stage. But for all the evidence of influence by his contemporaries' work, Southerne's collected plays display unique qualities particularly his own, qualities which we can trace in playwrights who came after him. Thus Southerne occupies a position straddling separate theatrical eras and yet seemingly apart from them. To understand this position more fully we must examine the particulars of Southerne's life and the milieu of the Restoration theater in which his work appeared.

I Southerne's Life and Times

Most of our information about the life of Thomas Southerne is preserved in the letters and biographical material of other men. Public records tell us that he was born in Dublin on February 12, 1659, to Francis and Margaret Southerne, educated at Trinity College, Dublin University, and admitted to the Middle Temple in London on July 15, 1680, presumably with an interest in studying law. He came to public attention first as a novice playwright under the auspices of the leading dramatist of the day, John Dryden, the poet laureate to King Charles II.

Southerne's first play, *The Loyal Brother, or, The Persian Prince,* appeared in 1682, ushered on and off the stage by a prologue and

15

epilogue by Dryden, two works more political than literary in tone. At the time Dryden was the leading spokesman for the Tory faction supporting the succession of James, Duke of York, to the throne. The occasion prompted an interchange between Dryden and Southerne which has become an oft-repeated literary anecdote and may have inspired Southerne in the commercial success he later achieved in the theater. Although they shared political sympathies, Dryden purportedly was not above taking advantage of his marketability at Southerne's expense. His occasional pieces for the theater were much in demand—indeed, they form a considerable part of his work. With Southerne's play Dryden raised his price, explaining he did so "not, young man, out of any disrespect to you, but the players have had my goods too cheap."[1] Southerne apparently felt the service worth the cost and had the advantage of a Dryden prologue for his second play as well when *The Disappointment, or, The Mother in Fashion* came out in 1684.

Both of Southerne's early plays were as successful on the stage as they might have been expected to be, given the uncertain circumstances of the time. The question of the succession to the throne had produced political unrest and factional rivalry between those who supported James, the Catholic heir apparent, and those who wished a Protestant successor to Charles; and resolution would not come until the end of the decade. In the theater the merger of the two licensed acting companies into one in 1682, shortly after the premiere of *The Loyal Brother*, diminished the range of production. Despite repetition of formulas and the continued writing of some leading figures, it was a period in which many careers and the theatrical tradition which had buoyed them up were coming to a close.

For Southerne, the early years of the 1680s were primarily a period of theatrical apprenticeship allowing him opportunity to test his powers on the stage and to experiment in the forms of drama that interested him. At the same time he was able, as both a dramatist and a Tory, to meet some of the leading theatrical figures of the day, notably such Tory writers as Dryden, Aphra Behn, Thomas Otway, and John Crowne. Although, with the exception of Dryden, we have no specific record indicating that Southerne had contact with any of these people, there can be little doubt that he did, given the smallness of the Restoration theater audience and the factionalism of theatrical people in the decade. Certainly the work Behn and Otway produced was to influence Southerne's later plays, as did Behn's novels when Southerne adapted them for the stage.

But for a long period in the decade Southerne's interests were not literary. In June 1685 he enlisted as an ensign in the Princess Anne's Regiment of the Duke of Berwick's Foot, eventually achieving command of a company.[2] However, his loyal service to James II ended when the king was deposed and succeeded by William III and Mary II, James's daughter. The resolution of the question of Protestant succession, settled firmly by the "Glorious Revolution" of 1688, despite generations of Jacobite plotting ahead, succeeded in shifting the attention of the public and the playwrights away from political factionalism back toward the kind of domestic concerns they had had a decade earlier. Leaving the army, Southerne sought to return to the theatrical world.

His initial attempt to renew his playwriting was begun a year before the Glorious Revolution, when he wrote four acts of *The Spartan Dame*, but its parallels with the current political situation, particularly its implied condemnation of the now victorious William, caused him to abandon it for a number of years. Instead Southerne returned to the theater in 1690 with *Sir Anthony Love, or, The Rambling Lady*, an outright comedy close in tone and setting to Aphra Behn's comedies of libertine intrigue, *The Rover* and *The Feign'd Curtizans*. The play was very successful and the next few years kept Southerne busy in efforts for the stage.

In large measure those years were a record of busy involvement with the literary world, most of it with Dryden and his circle, especially William Congreve. In the Princess Anne's Regiment Southerne had served with two cousins of Congreve, then a student at Trinity College.[3] Through the similarity of their backgrounds and the connections of Congreve's relatives, Congreve came to Southerne's attention after arriving in England and was introduced by him to Dryden. The three men remained close during the next decade, as Dryden indicated in a letter mentioning how Southerne and Congreve hiked out to meet him on his return to London so that they might travel the last few miles back in his company.[4] Their relationship extended into their dramatic work.

Although Southerne's *The Wives Excuse, or, Cuckolds Makes Themselves* was a failure on the stage when it appeared in 1691, it received high commendation from Dryden in an epistle printed with it. In the same year Dryden, who was ill, asked Southerne to help complete his tragedy *Cleomenes, the Spartan Hero*, his last successful play. Southerne also took Congreve's first play, *The Old Batchelor*, to Dryden, and the two of them, with Arthur Mainwaring, prepared it for the stage. It was produced and printed in 1693

with commendatory verses by Southerne, who proclaimed
Congreve the heir to Dryden. Southerne's bitter satire *The Maid's
Last Prayer, or, Any Rather than Fail* also appeared in 1693, with a
song by Congreve, generally regarded as his first work to appear on
the stage. In the same year Dryden, Southerne, and Congreve tentatively planned to write commendatory verses for a volume of
Wycherley's poems.[5] The following year Dryden advised Congreve,
whose *The Double Dealer* had received a lukewarm reception from
audiences, to model himself on Etherege, Southerne, and
Wycherley.

By now a regular circle had formed at Will's Coffeehouse around
Dryden and William Wycherley, the elder statesmen of the Restoration theater. Charles Hopkins, writing of that circle, which also included Congreve, Southerne, Anthony Hammond, Walter Moyle,
and himself, gives us a picture of Southerne as a man enjoying a
robust life: "In full delights let sprightly *Southern* live, / With all
that Women, and that Wine, can give."[6] In "To Anthony Hammond, Esq." Hopkins longs to rejoin the circle, "When you, and
Southerne, Moyle, and *Congreve* meet, / The best, good Men, with
the best-natur'd Wit."[7] The repetition of commendatory verses,
songs, epilogues, and references in letters suggests the closeness of
the circle and particularly the extensive involvement of the three
playwrights in each other's work.

After the stage failure of his two major comedies, Southerne
turned to tragedy. *The Fatal Marriage, or, The Innocent Adultery*,
in 1694, and *Oroonoko*, with an epilogue by Congreve, in 1695,
were resounding successes; in fact they were among the most
successful plays of the period. Together they established Southerne
as a major figure in the theater, and it is as the author of *Oroonoko*
and the creator of Isabella, the heroine of *The Fatal Marriage*, that
he was identified for the next century.

Yet Southerne's success did not alter his nature. As he had
assisted Congreve before, he continued to help aspiring
playwrights. One who provides an anecdote about the experience is
Colley Cibber, who began his career on the stage as a minor
character in *Sir Anthony Love* and later became an important
playwright and stage manager at Drury Lane. Cibber initially
received little encouragement for his first play, *Love's Last Shift, or,
The Fool in Fashion:*

However, Mr. *Southern*, the Author of *Oroonoko*, having had the Patience to hear me read it to him, happened to like it so well that he immediately recommended it to the Patentees, and it was accordingly acted in *January* 1695. In this play I gave myself the Part of Sir *Novelty*, which was thought, a good Portrait of the Foppery then in Fashion. Here, too, Mr. *Southern*, though he had approv'd my Play, came into the common Diffidence of me as an Actor: For, when on the first Day of it I was standing, myself, to prompt the *Prologue*, he took me by the Hand and said, *Young Man! I pronounce thy Play a good one; I will answer for its Success, if thou dost not spoil it by thy own Action.*[8]

The picture of Southerne that emerges here is that of a concerned and energetic supporter of young talent, a role he continued to play throughout his life. He wrote the prefatory dedication to Richard Norton's *Pausanias, The Betrayer of His Country*, published in 1696, and several other authors acknowledged his assistance in the writing and/or production of their plays, including John Dennis in the dedication of *Liberty Asserted* (1704), John Hughes in a letter regarding the production of *The Siege of Damascus* in 1719, and Elijah Fenton in the dedication to *Mariamne*, produced in 1723 but purportedly written at Southerne's house as early as 1711.[9] When Samuel Madden acknowledged his debt to Southerne in the preface to *Themistocles, The Lover of His Country* (1729), Fenton wrote that Southerne still "plays the bawd as formerly for the Muses."[10] Southerne's interest in younger writers extended long beyond his own period of theatrical activity.

These brief indications by others of Southerne's activities are typical of much of the information we possess about his life. More intimate and personal detail is harder to come upon. Yet from a few documents and contemporary references we can learn something of the course of Southerne's personal life. Sometime after the production of *Oroonoko*, he married Agnes Atkyns, a widow with two children. Little is known about their marriage, but a comment in the anonymous satire *Religio Poetae: or, A Satyr on the Poets* (1703) suggests that his wife was well-to-do. The author writes, "For since the Marriage-Yoke he has put on, / He drinks Champaign, and quits the Helycon."[11] The relative inactivity of Southerne after 1700, the sparse references to employment, the frequent reference to his visits and travels, all suggest that he enjoyed the life of a gentleman of leisure. By this and by some legal documents pertaining to financial matters, we can infer that he was a widower by 1731, when his own will was made out, making no mention of his wife but providing for his daughter.

The financial security of a wealthy wife and his own monetary theatrical success allowed Southerne to cease writing, but the impetus for abandoning his dramatic career might have come as much from other factors within the theater. In 1700 Dryden died and Southerne's first play in five years, *The Fate of Capua*, was not well received. Congreve, chafing from a lukewarm reception of *The Way of the World*, retired from the stage. Thus Southerne's closest associations, spanning the period of his greatest literary activity and his greatest success, were altered; and, when he himself stopped writing, the new century began with three of its strongest dramatic influences removed.[12]

Southerne lived forty-six years more, but his remaining theatrical work was slight. In 1719 he was finally able to bring an edited version of *The Spartan Dame* to the stage, with considerable success. His last play, *Money the Mistress*, produced in 1726, was not well received, however, and Southerne wrote no more drama. Typically, the writing of his final years was in connection with other playwrights. In the 1730s he provided biographical material on his friend Congreve,[13] and in 1745 he wrote a memoir of the theater in King Charles's time for the *Gentleman's Magazine*.[14]

Other than these works little is known of Southerne's life in the eighteenth century. He was involved in a controversy regarding his support of Dennis's pro-Whig play, *Liberty Asserted*, and lampooned for it in *The Tryal of Skill*, an anonymous poem published in 1704. He seems also to have taken employment as regimental agent for the Earl of Orrery's command and to have served as agent for at least two regiments at the same time. He was among a group of agents accused of shady conduct and resigned in 1714, having apparently added to the wealth acquired by his marriage and his playwriting.[15] Most references to Southerne are social, teasing him for his joviality or his growing deafness, or speaking warmly of his charm and sagacity. He is mentioned in the letters of Matthew Prior, Jonathan Swift, Congreve, Pope, William Broome, Elijah Fenton, Thomas Gray, and particularly his good friend John Boyle, Earl of Orrery. He was one of those to whom Pope sent his "pastorals" for critical advice, and he figures in poems by Pope, Prior, Gay, Fenton, Broome, and Defoe.

Southerne died on May 26, 1746. A poem on his death published in the *Gentleman's Magazine* for July 1746 gives us some indication of the reputation he left behind:

> Prais'd by the *grandsires* of the present age,
> Shall *Southern* pass unnoted off the stage?
> Who, more than half a century ago,
> Caus'd from each eye the tender tear to flow;
> Does not *his death* one grateful drop demand,
> In works of wit, the *Nestor* of our land?
> *Southern* was *Dryden's* friend: him genius warm'd,
> When *Otway* wrote, and *Betterton* perform'd.
> He knew *Poor Nat*, while regular his fire:
> Was *Congreve's* pattern, ere *he* rais'd desire:
> Belong'd to *Charles's* age, when wit ran high,
> And liv'd so long but to behold it *die*.[16]

II   *The Restoration Dramatic Tradition*

Southerne's best plays and his greatest theatrical activity occurred between 1690 and 1700, a decade of drama at the same time formulaic, transitional, and independent. "Restoration drama" has long been a general term for plays written between 1660 and the first decade of the eighteenth century (the closing date ranges from 1700 to 1710), but the term suggests more unity to the period than a study of its drama indeed supports. Actually there are a number of strands or currents flowing side by side. Several recent critics have pointed this out and attempted to outline the shifting movements within Restoration drama.[17]

It took some time for the theater in England to revive after the years of inactivity between the closing of the theaters in 1642 and the Restoration of Charles II. After a period dependent on revivals of earlier playwrights and borrowings from other sources, a body of work distinctive of Restoration playwrights began to emerge. The period between 1670 and 1680 was highly significant for the development of Restoration stage conventions of plot, character, and diction. In comedy this usually meant intrigues involving assignation or arranged marriage; witty, often libertine, young people pitted against avaricious and/or lecherous old people; and a tone of cynical, satiric wit. Etherege's *The Man of Mode* (1676), Wycherley's *The Country Wife* (1675) and *The Plain Dealer* (1676), Dryden's *Marriage a la Mode* (1672), Shadwell's *Epsom Wells* (1672) and *The Virtuoso* (1676), and Behn's *The Rover* (1677) and *Sir Patient Fancy* (1678) are examples of the variety of comedy within this period, offering a range of attitudes from moral indignation or satiric disgust to amoral delight over similar stage actions. At the same time heroic drama flourished, reaching its heights of energy and exuberance in Dryden's two-part *Conquest of Granada* (1672) and his *Aurenq-Zebe* (1675), and was transmuted into more regular tragedy by the end of the decade. Dryden's *All for Love* (1677), Lee's main body of work, including *Sophonisba* (1675) and *The Rival Queens* (1677), and Otway's *The Orphan* (1680) set the tone for a tragedy more concerned with exciting the passions than stirring the intellect.

The 1670s saw the development of the early Restoration's most successful and durable playwrights, figures whose works continued to be popular on the stage and to provide models for younger playwrights into the next century. But events of the 1680s inhibited the theater. The union of the two acting companies into one discouraged the production of new plays, and the political atmosphere, clouded by the question of the succession, cast a pall on the period. Some playwrights, like Shadwell, were driven from the stage by factional turmoil; others devoted much of their energy to the political debates; and still others, most notably Otway, found themselves turning against the main currents of Restoration drama with gloomy, hopeless tragedies and harsh, satiric comedies. However dynamic the 1670s had been, their major figures were gone by the end of the 1680s. Etherege, knighted and married, had long abandoned the stage; Wycherley, disgraced and impoverished, had spent long years in debtor's prison; Otway, Aphra Behn, and, after a period of confinement for madness, Lee all died in the decade. Dryden remained, his best work behind him, and Shadwell, after seven years away from the stage, returned with *The Squire of Alsatia* (1688), a play echoing the old comedy but pointing away from it. Thus, at a time when the Glorious Revolution replaced a Catholic king who represented the libertine court of the restored Stuart throne with a Protestant king and queen who vigorously and vocally encouraged public morality, the theater itself was ready to change direction.

This is not to suggest that the Restoration theater underwent a revolution. As Hume points out, the 1690s are a period of a double tradition in comedy, the hard, satiric, libertine comedy reviving and imitating earlier comedy and the gentler, moralistic, reforming comedy adding an element of exemplariness to romantic comedy.[18] Reforming comedy builds on romantic comedy and on a current of didactic comedy running intermittently throughout the previous decades. Shadwell and D'Urfey are early exponents. A considerably more rigid and intense treatment occurs in later plays by Cibber and Richard Steele in the 1700s.[19] For the first half of the decade these two strands of comedy were often found in the same plays, side by side, with no implied conflict, but by the close of the decade the satiric comedy had been softened and muted by the exemplary impulse.

We can recognize this shift by looking at one central concern of Restoration comedy, marriage conventions. As P. F. Vernon points out, the sexual intrigues of Restoration comedy, whether involving premarital or extramarital affairs, were in part expressing attitudes toward marriage conventions that these playwrights observed in their own society.[20] The marriage of convenience—arranged or "enforced" marriage—was widespread enough for the playwrights to see it as a common ill. Although for some it became merely a necessary plot device, several playwrights—notably Shadwell, Wycherley, Otway, and Behn—treated it as a serious evil. Most playwrights, these included, were content to satirize the results of such marriages through intrigues involving wanton wives and horned husbands; their most positive assertion was to suggest that matches for love were preferable to arranged marriages. Among these early Restoration playwrights, only Aphra Behn suggested a deeper concern for the distress and anguish of the women trapped in such marriages.[21]

But in the 1690s comedy gradually turned away from explicitly condoning sexual license, particularly adultery. Smith observes of *The Country Wake* (1696) that "in no English comedy thereafter (so far as I recall) was a hero to be permitted to make a cuckold in the progress of the play, and win the heroine also."[22] From Shadwell's *Squire of Alsatia* on, reformation of young rakes or errant spouses is a major motif in new plays. Cibber's *Love's Last Shift*, while retaining much of the atmosphere of libertine comedy, focuses on actions which reform a libertine husband and teach self-centered women to be good wives. The exemplary current becomes pervasive after Cibber's play. In play after play throughout the early decades of the eighteenth century, errant wives are specifically instructed to observe their duty to their marriage vows and to be faithful wives until their husbands, older men who acquired them in arranged marriages, die off. This view of the marital problem counteracts that of earlier Restoration comedy, but is no more satisfying. The effect would be finally to dissipate the comic conventions the later Restoration playwrights continued to draw upon, until they were replaced by conventions of quite a different kind of comedy. The disintegration of the attitude toward marriage as a social problem is one of the markers of the end of the kind of comedy peculiar to the Restoration. Marriage, while not the sole subject of Restoration comedy, nonetheless was central to its conventions and norms, and these in turn are what Southerne's comedies—and those influenced by him—respond to.

Restoration tragedy, too, developed its own peculiar conventions. Immediately after the Restoration, various strands or subgenres of serious drama—tragedy, heroic play, tragicomedy, historical play—were begun by new playwrights. Some wrote historical plays which disguised political comment on the late division of the kingdom; others wrote revenge tragedies modeled on Webster and Tourneur or borrowed and exaggerated Shakespearean characters and situations. But the most distinctive strand was the heroic play. Concerned with conflicts of love and honor and duty, usually plotted around the event of warfare (*The Siege of Rhodes, The Destruction of Jerusalem, The Conquest of China*), the heroic play directed itself toward the exciting of admiration in its audience. Dryden was particularly successful with the form but virtually every playwright who worked with any success in tragedy worked as well in heroic drama.

The decade of the 1670s began with great activity in heroic drama, but by 1680 important changes had occurred. Increasingly the interest in exciting the passions of the audience, so central to the Restoration view of tragic design, led to a treatment of character and of situation in isolation from theme and narrative consistency; dramatic "moments have individual meaning without contributing to an overall significance."[23] The gradually increased emphasis on the distress of the hero and the heroine made the later heroic play more concerned with pathos than with heroic virtues; this in turn directed the form toward "greater domesticity."[24] We can see this progression at work in the plays of the leading tragic dramatists of the 1670s. Dryden began the decade with the ambitious *Conquest of Granada,* centered on Almanzor, possibly the most active and vigorous Restoration hero, but *Aureng-Zebe,* his last heroic play, features a passive protagonist and *All for Love,* his best-known tragedy, depicts the distress of an heroic figure vacillating among a variety of demands upon his love.

Although there seems to be a clear distinction between Dryden's heroic plays and his tragedies, the distinction is not so clear when we try to isolate these forms in the work of other playwrights. Nathaniel Lee, John Banks, and Thomas Otway each began their careers in the 1670s with heroic plays which end not with the triumph of the hero over the obstacles set against him, or with a glorious defeat which makes his heroism seem triumphant, but with either suicide, madness, or death—that is, with antiheroic retreat or ignominious defeat rather than a triumph of any kind. Although such plays as Lee's *Sophonisba* (1675), Banks's *The Rival Kings* (1677), and Otway's *Don Carlos* (1676) are ostensibly about the same kind of conflicts which motivated the earlier heroic drama, they actually use public life as a foil against which to play private conflict. The personal desire for love, freedom of feeling, and happiness in a private world are continually thwarted or oppressed by the public world.

The concern with the pathetic and private marks the major tragedies of each of these writers. Lee's *The Rival Queens* (1677) is very close to *All for Love* in tone and theme, showing principally the private tragedy of a public figure. Banks wrought significant changes in the genre by returning to English history rather than the exotic locales of the Classical or Islamic world, and by developing the importance of female characters while avoiding the strident virility of the heroic male. *The Unhappy Favorite* (1681), though titled after the Earl of Essex, focuses on the distresses of Elizabeth I and Essex's wife. *Vertue Betrayed, or, Anna Bullen* (1682), *The Island Queens, or, The Death of Mary, Queen of Scots* (1684), and *The Innocent Usurper, or, The Death of Lady Jane Grey* (1683) all reveal their focus in their titles.[25] They demonstrate Banks's claim to having created the "she-tragedy." Otway's plays as well have significant female roles; Monimia in *The Orphan* and Belvidera in *Venice Preserved* (1682) are both victims of a corrupt male universe, although the victimization extends to males as well. Otway "carries to its psychological extreme the elements of passivity and introversion that the pathetic play involves."[26] He also provides the clearest example of domestic tragedy in *The Orphan*. Thus by the earlier part of the 1680s, the patterns of pathos, domesticity, emphasis on individual dramatic moments rather than unified totalities, are all significant features of Restoration tragedy, and the form of that tragedy remains the same when Southerne takes it up a decade later.

The 1690s, then, opened with strong traditions in comedy and tragedy already established. However, almost all the major figures of earlier Restoration drama were gone,[27] and while the repertory tradition kept the conventions of the earlier drama alive, the social and political circumstances which had produced that drama had dissolved. Restoration drama was born and shaped in the reign of Charles II, but that of James II provided little of the atmosphere or social ethos necessary to maintain its identity intact. With the ascension of William and Mary to the throne, and the emergence of the Whig party as the dominant political force, a new atmosphere settled over England, affecting the new drama being written. The political tensions of the 1680s transformed themselves into the social tensions of the 1690s and in a variety of ways the theater reflected that fact. A new generation of playwrights came to dominate the stage. In this decade Southerne wrote six of his ten plays, among them his best work, and at the same time Congreve and Vanbrugh wrote all of their original plays. After 1700 yet another group of playwrights emerged, and with Southerne and Congreve inactive, and Vanbrugh producing only translations, a change like that between the early and late Restoration occurred. The figures of the 1690s, so eminent in the history of Restoration drama, became as much part of the past as the shapers of Restoration drama had become before them.

III   *Southerne's Role in the Restoration Tradition*

Thomas Southerne's first two plays, *The Loyal Brother* and *The Disappointment*, products of the early 1680s, were largely apprentice work from the standpoint of the later drama, and the period of their composing was significant from Southerne's position more because of his contacts with leading dramatists and the theatrical world than because of his actual achievement. But in the last decade of the seventeenth century he was able to produce a body of plays building upon and enhancing the Restoration comic and tragic traditions. Furthermore, both his comedies and his tragedies showed common elements of theme and characterization.

The interest in the plight of the distressed heroine, demonstrated in his first play and made more dominant and domestic in his second, is a prominent aspect of Southerne's writing, distinguishing him from his contemporaries. *The Wives Excuse* is a multi-level portrayal of the victimization of women by a predatory, male-dominated society. It drew heavily upon the conventions of character and plot common to earlier libertine comedy, but its sym-

pathy with the beleaguered women demonstrates a reforming intention. Many critics have had difficulty accepting Southerne's clash of
tone with convention; much of the critical neglect of the play is due
to the tendency of scholars to view Restoration comedy
monolithically, looking at its conventions and overlooking how it
realigns them. The contemporary audience had the same difficulty;
The Wives Excuse was a stage failure, Southerne believed, because
its audience could not accept his violation of stage conventions.
Indeed, the continuance of a double tradition of satiric and exemplary comedy into the eighteenth century shows that audiences
could accept the conventions of either tradition, often side by side
in a single play, but they tolerated subversions of these traditions
with great reluctance. Libertine comedies like *The Man of Mode*
and *The London Cuckolds* continued to share the stage with
moralistic fables like *Love's Last Shift* or *The Careless Husband*,
but *The Wives Excuse*, which used the conventions of libertine
comedy—the foolish husband, the cunning rake, the sex intrigues—to attack the principles which that comedy seemed to uphold, failed because it subverted those conventions.[28]
    In addition to its stagecraft, *The Wives Excuse* was notable in
another way. It accepted the dramatic presupposition that arranged
marriage produced only frustration and cynicism but added depth
by seriously sympathizing with the dilemma of an intelligent and
honorable woman trapped in a hopeless marriage. By accepting
conventions of character while avoiding caricature or stock
characterization, in effect Southerne went beyond Aphra Behn's
recurrent sniping to produce a frontal assault. That "cuckolds make
themselves" is implicit in the play (and explicit in the title), but
Southerne analyzed the undersurface of that cliché and went on to
propose that a wife's infidelity is not a satisfying solution to the
problem of such a marriage nor is the complicity in adultery by a
complacent society a sufficient response to a situation more demanding of sympathy than amusement.
    Southerne's point may have been lost on the theater audience,
but its impact was still to be felt among the reading public. The
Gentleman's Journal recommended reading the play.[29] So did
Dryden, whose commendatory verses to Southerne were printed
with it, and certainly it was read by all the leading wits and
playwrights, particularly those of Dryden's circle at Will's
Coffeehouse. His praise of Southerne, comparing him to Terence,
was not lost on them.
    Within the next few years marriage was treated in a small body of

plays in a way it had not been treated before. Congreve's *The Dou-ble Dealer*, his second play, was a harsh attack on adultery and marriages of convenience, and Crowne's *The Married Beau, or, The Curious Impertinent* (1694), following the theme of Southerne's *The Disappointment*, was an insightful and disturbing analysis of the libertine sensibility, exploring the central triangle of Southerne's play in far greater depth than Southerne himself had. The dilemma of Mrs. Friendall, Southerne's distressed heroine, who is honorable enough to withstand temptation but human enough to feel it, is treated again in Vanbrugh's *The Provoked Wife* (1697), the most thorough and perceptive analysis of marriage in the period. Farquhar's *The Beaux' Stratagem* (1707) duplicates Van-brugh's marriage triangle but adds a good deal of argument, borrowed from John Milton's *Defense of Divorce* (1645), that marriages and divorces ought to be governed by the consent of the principals, rather than the will of the parents or the state. Moreover, the central focus of Congreve's rich and delightful *The Way of The World* (1700) is an exploration of the effect of adultery on the con-duct and aspirations of a kaleidoscope of couples.[30]

This group of plays, this comedy of marriage, is distinguished by its treatment of the marriage theme. As A. H. Scouten has observed, "in terms of the historical approach, the significant play in this group is *The Wives Excuse*," in large part because it is the first to shift "from the unmarried 'gay couple' to the problems of a married couple."[31] We should also note that these plays are among the most highly regarded of the period, those most often anthologized, studied, and revived. Moreover, even the plays which pull against Southerne's realistic approach to the marriage problem are none-theless indebted to him for raising it. Cibber's *Love's Last Shift*, with its conservative idealism about marriage, is trying to offer an exemplary model of what marriage should be, much as Congreve and the others are attempting more naturalistic or satiric examina-tion. Vanbrugh's response to Cibber, *The Relapse, or, Virtue in Danger* (1696), Cibber's later *The Careless Husband* (1701) and *The Lady's Last Stake* (1707), and Cibber's revision of Vanbrugh's fragment *A Journey to London* as *The Provoked Husband* (1723) are in keeping with this exemplary line of development. A number of plays imitating either Cibber or Vanbrugh thus respond to Southerne's original impulse.

Southerne himself, however, did not follow in the mode of *The Wives Excuse*. His next play, *The Maid's Last Prayer*, was one of the harshest satires of the period. As if following Dryden's admonition to copy Wycherley, he produced here a play as hard as *The Country Wife* or *The Plain Dealer*, as hard even as Otway's gloomy, cynical comedies, *The Soldier's Fortune* and *The Atheist*. Southerne takes the libertine comic conventions to their extremes here, and the resulting harshness was more than the audience could accept. But we should note that a similar seriousness of tone pervades *The Double Dealer*, which Dryden compared to the best of Etherege, Southerne, and Wycherley. Significantly, with that play Congreve had to defend himself against misinterpretation just as Southerne did with *The Wives Excuse*.[32]

Although the effects of Southerne's comedies were to reverberate in the works of others, he himself moved into tragedy, bringing a new perspective to themes running through his earlier plays. *The Fatal Marriage* offers a picture of a distressed heroine who, beset by a greedy and insensitive society, is unwittingly led into adultery, madness, and death. Isabella, one of the best-known heroines of the succeeding century and a half, resembles both Otway's Monimia, the victim of a perverse landscape in *The Orphan*, and his own Mrs. Friendall, placed in an extreme position. Southerne's play is even more of a domestic tragedy than Otway's and points the way toward the domestic tragedies of Rowe and Lillo in the next century. Although Rowe's she-tragedies concentrate on suffering heroines like Lady Jane Grey or Jane Shore and deal with fallen innocents rather than purer souls like Southerne's heroines, they share a sense of sympathy with the woman's role in the world. Calista, in *The Fair Penitent* (1703), echoes Southerne's Mrs. Friendall when she laments the "hard condition of our sex, / Through ev'ry state of life the slaves of men."[33] Southerne's presence is felt here, and the continued success of *The Fatal Marriage* and his succeeding tragedy, *Oroonoko*, on stage throughout the century kept that presence continually accessible.

Thus the eighteenth century opened with strong influences emanating from Southerne's work. How powerfully they affected the work of Congreve, his most important protégé, or Cibber, whose best work is often antithetical to Southerne's and Congreve's, is hard to measure. Certainly the other choices for his patronage of whom we are sure, Richard Norton, John Dennis, Elijah Fenton, and Samuel Madden, produced no theatrical works of great significance; and, with the exception of Dennis, an admirer of Dryden, their careers were not closely tied to the theater.

Nonetheless every great name in literature in his lifetime knew and respected either Southerne or his work. Isabella and Oroonoko each left an indelible impression on all who saw them portrayed on the stage. Although Southerne's direct role in the theater, measured by the number of plays produced or the duration of his career, was not great, his impact was surely felt upon the foremost dramatists of his time, and his work itself merits a close appraisal and a thorough reading.

CHAPTER 2

The Early Plays

THE decade of the 1680s was a period in which Southerne learned his craft. The two plays he produced in the reign of Charles II are marked by a multitude of influences—Shakespeare, Dryden, heroic drama, political issues, to name the most obvious. His friendship with Dryden and the Tory writers undoubtedly led to associations with such figures as Thomas Otway and Aphra Behn, both of whom influenced his later work and were at the top of their careers when he arrived in London. Yet, for all the influences we find, something distinctly Southerne appears in these plays, a sympathy with the suffering heroine, particularly when her distress is related to marriage, an interest in marriage itself, and a tendency to analyze and complicate his characters and to present conflict in a continuum rather than in distinct opposition. In a variety of ways, the elements which are the hallmarks of Southerne's major plays, written a decade later, appear first in the plays which begin his theatrical career.

I The Loyal Brother

The date of the premiere of Southerne's first play, *The Loyal Brother, or, The Persian Prince,* while not known for certain, must have been close to the date the king first saw it as a new play, February 4, 1682.[1] Publication followed in four months. The prologue and epilogue, both written by Dryden and capitalizing upon the play's political implications, were printed separately, as part of the continuing war of words between Whig and Tory propagandists, and suggest that Dryden was interested in this play primarily as a political vehicle. Certainly it was only one of several plays of markedly political bias in the period.[2]

Appropriateness to the current political situation affected Southerne's treatment of the material from which he drew the play. His source was *Tachmas, Prince of Persia: An Historical Novel,*

31

Which Happened Under the Sophy Seliman, Who Reigns at this Day, an English translation of a French novel, published in 1676.[3] The story of Tachmas is a personal tragedy in the novel, but Southerne's play offers the conflicts in political terms as well and resolves them happily.

The Loyal Brother centers on the threat against the love of Prince Tachmas and Semanthe for one another and the dangers to their lives caused by the machinations of three villains: Ismael, an ambitious counselor to the Sophy of Persia; Arbanes, a disaffected general resentful of Tachmas's military prowess; and Sunamire, Arbanes's sister, made vengeful by unrequited love for Tachmas. Their conspiring consists primarily of making Seliman suspect Tachmas's loyalty, resent his popularity with the people, and desire the woman Tachmas loves. A hurried plot leads Seliman to suspect Tachmas of conspiring for the throne and to sentence him to die on the scaffold, but he relents when his mother and Semanthe persuade him of Tachmas's innocence. A second plot then produces a forged letter which leads Semanthe to doubt Tachmas's love and Seliman to imprison him again for treason. While Ismael leads an abortive revolt of the rabble, Arbanes and Sunamire confront Semanthe and Tachmas in prison, revealing their own misdeeds and attempting to poison the lovers. Through the intervention of Osman, a soldier loyal to Tachmas, Arbanes and Sunamire die instead. Ismael is led out to die and Seliman surrenders Semanthe to his brother.

This outline of events offers little of political significance. Whatever else Southerne hoped to achieve in this play, he is clearly building on the tradition of heroic and pathetic drama already well established in Restoration theater. The very setting in the reign of Sulieman or Seliman relates it to the earliest heroic drama, Davenant's *The Siege of Rhodes* or Orrery's *The Tragedy of Mustapha*, both drawn from histories of Sulieman. Character equivalences exist between Southerne's play and both Dryden's *Aureng-Zebe* and Otway's *Don Carlos* (1676), and all three share, in varying degrees, a concern with the pathetic rather than heroic elements of the form. The general similarity of most of these plays, the closeness of Southerne's play to its source, and the modifications of plot Southerne introduced for political purposes all suggest that those equivalences are more coincidental than directly derivative.[4]

Restoration serious drama did not exist in rigid categories.[5] If we say this play is more heroic than some others, that play more tragic, such descriptions arise more from a shift in emphasis among similar material than from a radical dissimilarity of incompatible elements. Moreover, the pathos so necessary to Restoration high tragedy is inherent in heroic drama from the beginning. *The Loyal Brother,* written after the chief works of Lee, Banks, and Otway, is far closer in tone to pathetic tragedy than to heroic drama, and the directions it takes away from heroic form reveal the degree to which Southerne perceived the play in other terms.

The political element of the play is one factor that influences its direction. The parallel of a king whose counselors seek to turn him against his brother and heir with the attempts of the Whigs to block the succession of the Catholic James by forcing Charles to name a Protestant heir is obvious and clear.[6] But although the plot has been crafted to enhance similarities with the political issues, its effectiveness as a political weapon is minimal. Beyond exhorting the king to trust his brother and distrust his counselors the play avoids political reality. Other than his final benevolence, little in Seliman recommends him as a model to Charles II; he is shown at times to be vain, self-aggrandizing, gullible, and selfish. To reduce the question of the succession to petty jealousy and conflicts of sexual interest is simply to depoliticize it. Indeed, Rothstein, using this play as an example, has pointed out that in the later heroic play "political interests remain subordinate and, despite censors' pens and prologues' demagoguery, political allusions in Restoration tragedy almost never do more than add spice or set norms in an otherwise conventional and apolitical plot."[7] Thus while *The Loyal Brother* has clear correspondences to actual figures in a real situation, it is, Dryden's factional prologue and epilogue notwithstanding, far less pointed and dedicated a piece of propaganda than, for example, Dryden's own brilliant *Absalom and Achitophel.*

Political questions are never prominent in any of Southerne's plays, nor is the heroism and villainy of Restoration serious drama, even in this play. Instead, he is much more involved with the responses of men and women to domestic crisis. His concern with private lives in turmoil, appearing in his earliest play, foreshadows the events and interests of his finest work in comedy and tragedy and betrays the influence of more serious and introspective drama than heroic plays.

The first major influence comes from Dryden. Seliman in all his shifting passion, swayed by counselors, family, love, and honor, very much resembles the tortured Antony of *All for Love,* nowhere

more clearly than in the emotional scaffold scene which closes Act
III. There Seliman is physically held in place and morally besieged
by Semanthe and his mother, Begona, who beg him, kneeling, to
spare Tachmas's life. Here is the final barrage:

> Beq.   O! I conjure you, pity my complainings
>   And give my *Tachmas* to these falling tears.
> Sem.   By fame!
> Beq.   By nature, by your father's dust!
> Sem.   By the bright throne of *Cyrus!*
> Beq.   By the sun,
>   And all those stars, that ever blest this land
>   With their auspicious influence!
> Sem.   He yields, he melts, I read it in his looks:
>   A blush confus'dly wanders in his cheeks;
>   And now he turns away. O blessed change!
> Beq.   O matchless virtue! happy, happy day!
>
>   . . .
>
> Sel.   —O rise, my royal mother! rise, *Semanthe!*
>   Yes, you have conquer'd, and I blush to think
>   I could so long resist such wond'rous virtue.
>   (44)

The structure of this moment is very like that in *All for Love* where
Antony in silence bears the assault of family and friend and caves in
tearfully.[8] In each case the scene is built around supplication and a
resolution caused by emotion rather than reason. Nor is the scene in
either case especially dependent upon previous characterization,
although susceptibility to emotion is Antony's chief characteristic.
Even though Southerne's scene is more detached from the fabric of
the play than Dryden's, the presentation suggests a similarity
Southerne saw between the circumstances of the two characters.

The second significant influence is Shakespearean. As much as
Seliman resembles Antony in Dryden's play, he also resembles
Othello in Shakespeare's tragedy, particularly in scenes with the
villain, Ismael, who is very similar to Iago.[9] Southerne's debt is particularly clear in the third scene of Act II where Ismael works upon
Seliman's suspicions by indirection, prompting Seliman to "force" a
"reluctant" Ismael to give information about Semanthe and
Tachmas that incites the Sophy to rage, much as Othello is driven to
murderous rage by Iago in Act III of *Othello*. Ismael also speaks
often in soliloquy, sharing his villainy with the audience just as Iago

does. Of course, Ismael's villainy has a political dimension to it that Iago's doesn't, yet even the difference is Shakespearean. The rabble, drunken citizens and wanton wives, appear in two scenes. In the second Ismael rouses them to revolution in the same way Antony wins over the populace in *Julius Caesar*. He begins:

> My worthy countrymen! my fellow-suffers!
> To you I come to weep this kingdom's tears,
> To sigh its groaning sorrows out and pour
> Into your ears its sad calamities:
>
> (58 - 59)

and leads them to believe that the oppressive Sophy has murdered Tachmas:

> He was your guard, your shield; but now is gone:
> He fell because he lov'd you, and will you
> Not solemnize his funeral in blood?
> Will you stand here, like statues, motionless,
> Weep o'er his gaping wounds, and not revenge 'em?
>
> (60)

This scene and the other rabble scene are the clearest politically motivated additions to the play. They satirize the folly of democratic rule, as well as the attempt by Shaftesbury to build a solid political base among the populace. Yet they also demonstrate that artistically Southerne turned to Shakespeare repeatedly as his model, rather than to more contemporary treatments of crowd scenes such as appear intermittently in earlier heroic drama.

Shakespearean indebtedness also appears in the characterization of Tachmas. Although we hear of Tachmas's off-stage valor, on stage we never see him in heroic postures. For the most part he is passive, more acted upon than acting. Although he and Arbanes duel, the final deaths of the villains are attributable to accidental self-poisoning. The particularly Shakespearean side of Tachmas's nature is revealed when he is distressed and suffering. Then he becomes as meditative as Hamlet and, in fact, his speeches echo Hamlet's soliloquies. In III, iv, the scaffold scene, he meditates on death:

> Death we should prize, as the best gift of nature,
> As a safe inn, where weary travellers,

When they have journied through a world of cares,
May put off life, and be at rest for ever . . .

                    . . .

Then why should I delay? or fondly fear
To embrace this soft repose, this last retreat?
I? who like blossoms withering on the bough,
Dy'd in my birth, and almost was born old.
                                                    (40)

Here and elsewhere Tachmas's role is primarily static, con-
templative, and introspective. In these moments Southerne draws
upon Shakespearean models, as he does in several other scenes
already mentioned. Thus the scaffold scene, although it is modeled
on the scene in the novel, is heightened in its impact when
Southerne makes it not merely a highly dramatic moment but an in-
tensely thought-provoking one. Unfortunately, however, as well as
Southerne handles the soliloquy here, it is difficult to place it in the
context of the play or to avoid comparing it with its original. In
either case the moment falters.

In this respect we can see what is most typically Restoration
about this play: the emphasis on single moments rather than
cohesiveness and total coherence. Stroup has pointed out the
reference to Descartes in Act IV where "Tachmas, 'discovering'
himself, to his philosophical consternation, in prison, ruminates: 'I
think therefore am: hard state of man! / That proves his being with
an argument / That speaks him wretched.' "[10] The paraphrase of
Descartes identifies Tachmas (or Southerne) as familar with the
philosopher, but the soliloquy is less an intellectual exploration of
the implications of that thought in these circumstances than a
stepping-off place for self-conscious pathetic appeal regarding his
distress. Here, as elsewhere in this play, the moment, however
heightened by intellectual or emotional power, serves chiefly to
magnify the audience's empathy with the character at that time. All
these dark musings notwithstanding, the ending of the play is
positive. Right conquers wrong, the happy couple are united, justice
prevails—all in contradiction to the novel, which ends with
Tachmas's blinding and murder, Sunamire's madness, confession,
and suicide, Negare (Semanthe in the play) and Begone killing
themselves for grief, and Allagolikan (Ismael) strangled before
Seliman's eyes, all in a couple of pages.

If these moments seem typical and derivative, there is nonetheless much about *The Loyal Brother* which is characteristic of Southerne's chief interests in drama. Semanthe, the suffering and hard-pressed heroine, is the first of Southerne's portraits of women in distress, a central motif of his work. She is an heroic figure as a heroine—faithful, courageous, single-minded. In the novel upon which the play is based, the Semanthe character for a time considers submitting to the Sophy for the wealth and power she would attain. As Dodds observes, "such a character was too complex to fit the conception of the play, which called for a heroine who could suffer and endure, but on whose faithfulness there must be no stain. The steadfast love of Southerne's Semanthe never wavered; she could spurn a crown without regret."[11] Consequently Semanthe is an ideal rather than a real figure. Yet Southerne would return to such plot developments as a suffering heroine or beset lovers, in far more realistic ways, time and time again. As we will see, these elements are strongly tied to the persistent themes of his works and, by comparison, reveal how that work matured and focused over the years.

As for the play itself, it remains an interesting amalgam of various themes and motifs of Restoration serious drama. John Harold Wilson included it among the still readable heroic tragedies.[12] Although Dodds thought the play lacked "dramatic integrity as a whole," even he admitted it was effective in the scaffold scene.[13] Knight called the execution scene "spectacular" and wrote that the "attack against brutality is characteristic, Southerne's tendency being to stress the warmer, gentler emotions. . . . His poetry's emotional disposition is indicated by the good Tachmas' expression of willingness to 'offer the scarlet treasure of my heart' (III, iv)."[14] Summers called it "a very fine piece of work which, one is able to be glad to record, achieved a great success."[15] A month after its first performance, however, the Theatre Royal closed and the United Company was formed. There is no record of its being performed again after that initial run.

II The Disappointment

Southerne's second play, *The Disappointment, or, The Mother in Fashion,* must have appeared on the stage for the first time in late March or early April of 1684. The prologue by Dryden and the epilogue were separately printed on April 5. It is a play quite different from *The Loyal Brother,* particularly in tone. The title page simply calls it a play, but it is deeply marked by borrowings from both Shakespearean tragedy and Restoration comedy, and may best be described as a domestic drama. It consists of two lines of action, each supportive of the other, with several characters moving between them.

The principal action is influenced by the story of the curious impertinent in *Don Quixote*.[16] There, a man's suspicion of his wife instigates a testing of her fidelity by their friend, her ultimate fall, and tragic consequences for all three principals. Southerne considerably alters the story, particularly its outcome. The attempts of Alberto to seduce Erminia, wife of Alphonso, lead Alphonso to believe her false. Indeed, Alberto himself believes he has been successful, little knowing that he has in fact enjoyed his cast mistress, Juliana. Even Lorenzo, Alphonso's loyal friend and the spokesman for calm reason in the play, suspects Erminia because of the evidence against her. But ultimately the mistake is revealed, in time to prevent Alphonso from killing his wife in a jealous rage after he has already wounded Alberto.

The secondary action of the play loosely parallels the principal plot. Alberto seeks to seduce Angelline, Rogero's daughter and Lorenzo's beloved, through the agency of her supposed mother. Once again Juliana substitutes for the intended victim in bed and there is confusion over whom Alberto has actually seduced. Ultimately the truth is revealed and a repentant Alberto takes back Juliana, Rogero gives Angelline to Lorenzo, and the mother is revealed to be Rogero's mistress, Angelline's mother having died when she was an infant.

In its almost geometric arrangement of happy endings *The Disappointment* resembles a good many Elizabethan domestic dramas, but the change Southerne has wrought in familiar material demonstrates a consistency of purpose in the parallel plots of the play and an advance in Southerne's control of "dramatic integrity" in his work. Far more successfully than in *The Loyal Brother*, Southerne has integrated his influences into the context of the play.

Most of the ways in which the original curious impertinent story is altered by Southerne are made consistent by tone and action borrowed from Shakespeare. Cervantes's jealous husband, whose overcuriosity artificially creates a situation which destroys his marriage and leads him to suicide, his wife to a convent, and his friend to death in war, takes on overtones not only of Othello, a rather inevitable comparison, but also of Hamlet.[17] Like Othello, Southerne's Alphonso is driven to murderous rage: he conspires to

kill the Duke of Florence when he thinks him responsible for Erminia's seduction, actually stabs Alberto, and attempts to kill his
wife. Like Othello, too, he speaks of the bliss of ignorance:

> She might have numbred out the Stars in Sin;
> Fed her hot, lustful Appetite with Change
> Of every high-fed, wanton Fool in *Florence;*
> Yet I been happy:
>
> . . .
>
> But to know myself a Monster! Death and Hell!
> Children and Fools will have me in the Wind,
> And I shall stink of Cuckold to the World.
>   (87)

Throughout the play Alphonso shifts and switches, now jealous and
nearly insane with anger, now compassionate and forgiving, now
secretive and murderous. Like Othello, his portrait is of a manic
personality, a jealous man obsessed by his humor.

Alphonso's Hamlet-like qualities are not so well integrated into
this domestic portrait, partly because his motives for behaving like
Hamlet are not central to the actual circumstances of the plot. Like
Hamlet Alphonso feigns madness while waiting for an opportunity
for revenge, and his dialogues with Rogero, a bluff, direct old man,
directly echo those of Hamlet and Polonius. But even though they
are effective scenes in themselves, as are Alphonso's soliloquies
about his feigned madness, they are misplaced in the play. The
Duke is in fact never a character onstage and only peripherally a
character offstage. Alphonso is soon redirected toward the actual
culprit, Alberto. Yet as much as the misdirection may be for isolated
effect, it also cues us to Southerne's ruling principle of characterization. Here his interest is not so much in tragedy or even tragedy *in
posse* but rather in the close analysis of character under stress.

To this end it is important that Erminia, like Desdemona, be
chaste and passive, one who suffers and endures rather than
responds or retaliates. When Alphonso abandons her, Erminia tells
Lorenzo that Heaven will witness "how I ever liv'd, and always
will, / (Tho' banisht from his Sight and Bed for ever) / His truly
loving and obedient Wife" (119). The hope of pardon by her husband makes her trust that "all my past Misfortunes did but
prove / The Purgatory to this Heav'n of Love" (124). In such

speeches Erminia seems the type of Patient Griselda, who endures all wrongs without rebellion, trusting in her husband's right and wisdom. Didactic domestic drama previously in the century had continually offered such a model wife.[18] But Southerne is not simply repeating the stereotype. In this play, as in others by Southerne, woman is seen principally as a victim of predatory men, and Erminia's passiveness as a wife both deepens the pathos of her suffering—not only is she wronged but she also is willing to be martyred rather than return wrong—and heightens the injustice and insensitivity of the men. Her characterization is the central portrayal of distressed womanhood, but the characterizations of all the women serve that end.

Just as Erminia is the model of the chaste wife, Angelline (as her name implies) is the model of the chaste maiden. The subplot in which she is involved has clear equivalences in Shakespeare's *All's Well That Ends Well*. Angelline is like the chaste Diana, Juliana like the wronged Helena, Alberto like the wayward Bertram.[19] Like Diana, Angelline's chief role is to preserve her innocence and resist the seductive power of the rake. Yet even with the bawd-mother assisting in her seduction, she is never in real danger because of the presence of Juliana, who has already worked the bedroom switch in the marriage plot.

Juliana is a pivotal character in the play, a replacement both for Cervantes' servant, Leonela, whose visits by her lover originally spark the husband's suspicions, and also for one of the twins in Behn's *The Amorous Prince*, where mistaken identity creates suspense. In *The Disappointment*, as in earlier variations of the bed switch, the woman who takes the intended female's place is tied to the man involved by previous sexual intimacy; the bed switch leads to a legitimatizing of that relationship. But Juliana is also the weak woman, the cast mistress, who lacks the moral character and strength of purpose of either Erminia or Angelline, and who, if she had it to do again, would fall just as before. However, Southerne presents her wholly in sympathetic terms, as an example of where but for their own strength of character, Erminia and Angelline would be. Whereas they are victims of men *in posse*, she is one in actuality.

Even further fallen away from the chaste ideal are the bawd-mother of Angelline and the easily bribed Clara, Erminia's maid, both examples of women corrupted by men and made servants to the predatory male. But neither of these portraits is wholly unsympathetic: the bawd-mother has the justification of her relationship with Rogero, and Clara is given the opportunity to redeem herself by assisting Juliana and foiling Alberto.

The women have in common their potential or past victimization by the men; the men share a trait among themselves: an inherent skepticism of the faithfulness of women. Alberto uses this attitude to justify his sexual predations when he tells his friend Lesbino in I, i:

> For me, I'm settled in my Faith: I've made
> A study of the Sex, and found it frail:
> The black, the brown, the fair, the old, the young,
> Are earthly-minded all: There's not a She,
> The coldest Constitution of the Sex,
> Nay, at the Altar, telling o'er her Beads,
> But some one rises on her heav'nly thoughts,
> That drives her down the wind of strong Desire,
> And makes her taste Mortality again.
>
> (84)

Alberto is the archetypal Restoration rake and the opening scene of the play presents him exactly as Etherege's Dorimant and Wycherley's Horner are displayed, at home, delighting in themselves and basking in the admiration of friends. His view of women is also typical of the rake, and, when he repents later in the play, it is this heresy he rejects.

Alberto may speak the heresy, but it is a shared notion of all the men in the play. Alphonso's obsessive and dangerous response to the suggestion of his wife's infidelity is as much motivated by erroneous preconceptions of feminine frailty as is Alberto's cynical libertinism. Even Lorenzo, the calm, clear-headed friend who continually struggles to make Alphonso rule his passions, for a moment thinks that Erminia has been unchaste with Alberto and castigates her for it. Although he is quick to see his error, he nonetheless is susceptible to the same failing as the other men.

But the worst offender is really Rogero, whom Southerne has made the embodiment of the male double standard. Although he is very protective of his daughter and suspicious of the motives of the men around her, he nonetheless is in sympathy with the predatory male instinct. After he has learned that Alphonso made no advances to Angelline when they were alone together, he still questions her: "Why, what a Pox, neither kiss, tickle or tumble, fumble or mumble you? What, did he not offer you Testimony of his Manhood, Child? . . . A Man may do that in a civil way to show his Breeding, Child; That he may, and no harm done" (140). We see how much this double standard has permeated his life at the end of the play, when Lorenzo expresses hesitation over the influences of the mother on the daughter he wishes to marry. Rogero reveals that the mother is

> no Matrimonial Consort of mine, but the natural
> Iniquity of my Youth.
>
> Lor.   Your Whore!
>
> Roq.   My Concubine, an't please you. (150 - 51)

The distinction is slight but important to Rogero, since his name for her elevates her position and his. When the "Concubine" asks his pardon, he replies, "Why, what did I set you up for, but to follow your Trade? I know a Whore runs as naturally into a Bawd, as a young Man into Letchery and the Pox." Rogero takes her back but his view of her and of women in general is still cynical, operating in total indifference to his initial role in turning her from maiden to "whore." In fact, Rogero's cyncism, for all his protectiveness of his daughter, is not far from Alberto's own.

Rogero remains the embodiment of the double standard, the only man who doesn't learn from the experience of the play. But the testing of Erminia and Angelline does affect the other male characters. Juliana's behavior, Alberto tells her, "has subdu'd my Wilder Thoughts and fix'd me only Thine." His regrets over his attempts on Angelline and Erminia make him a model of the reformed rake; accepting his cast mistress is emblematic of his rejection of his earlier cynical opinion. The virtuous heroines have proved him wrong.

Alphonso, of course, is the major learner in the play and pronounces the moral of the main plot:

> And Innocence is prov'd; Oh there's the thing.
> For 'tis a Woman's falsest, vainest Pride,
> To boast a Virtue, that has ne'er been try'd:
> —In equal Folly too those Husbands live,
> Who peevishly against themselves contrive
> By early Fears, to hasten on the Day:
> For Jealousie but shews our Wives the Way:

> And if the forked Fortune be our Doom,
> In vain we strive; The Blessing will come home.
> (151)

In a later play, *The Wives Excuse*, Southerne will return in a more complex way to the theme that Alphonso announces, the guilt of the husband in the wife's infidelity. Significantly, in this play no guilt attaches to the wife at all. Where other playwrights took delight in the horning of the errant or foolish husband, as Wycherley does in *The Country Wife* or Aphra Behn does in several plays, Southerne is reluctant to let his wives put into practice what the morality of the play and of the comic conventions of Restoration comedy cheerfully accept.

Dodd saw *The Disappointment* as a "play verging closely on the sentimental, moralizing drama of Cibber and Steele" and believed it to be "extremely significant, for it shows [Southerne] taking the formulae of Restoration comedy and adding to them something of his own that points forward to his main achievement in the theatre—the development of a sentimental problem drama."[20] While Southerne's main achievement may arguably be something else, certainly here he has borrowed from the traditions of Restoration comedy, particularly in the character of Alberto and in the concern of both plots with sexual adventure, and used them for his own purposes. His treatment of the material is significant as well since it is part of a body of plays extolling marriage and female virtue at a time when so much Restoration comedy is cynical and libertine in tone. However, it is not so utterly didactic as a play like D'Urfey's *The Virtuous Wife, or, Good Luck at Last* (1679). Rather it is closer to the biting comedy of Behn and Otway, however less gloomy and cynical it appears to be. It *is* a problem drama, and Southerne shows himself to be far more interested in the personal ramifications of the situation for the characters than in the social situation they reflect.

Little is known of the play's success, except that it was played for the king and queen on January 27, 1685, ten days before Charles's death.

CHAPTER 3

Sir Anthony Love

I *Theatrical Background, Sources, and Influences*

THE premiere date of *Sir Anthony Love, or, The Rambling
Lady* is not known. The title page reads 1691, and the Term
Catalogues have an entry for its publication in February 1691. The
production was advertised in the *London Gazette* for December 18 -
22, 1690, and, conjecturing from this data and patterns of performance and publication, Milhous and Hume tentatively assign the
premiere to November 1690.[1] The play seems to have been very
successful.

Sir Anthony Love offers a radical change of pace from the kind of
drama that Southerne had been writing, not only because it is his
first comedy but because it lacks the unity of design evident in his
early plays. Although we may say that Southerne consistently has
problems weaving together all the elements he wishes a play to con-
tain, he nonetheless is able to produce one or two plots which advance characterization and theme. Here, however, the diverse
fragments with which he began remain fragmented. While we can
get some sense of what he is about by examining the separate
strands of action, producing a cohesive, coherent whole is difficult
in the play.

Robert Jordan has identified the source of one of the chief plots as
The Lucky Mistake (1689), one of the last novels by Aphra Behn.[2]
In this plot Count Canaille (Behn's De Pais), a Frenchman of
Spanish strictness, decides to marry his older daughter, Floriante
(Atlante), to Count Verole (Vernole in the novel), and places his
younger daughter, Charlott, in a nunnery. Floriante loves Valentine
(Rinaldo); however, when Valentine is set upon by Verole's bravos,
the distressed father sends Floriante to the nunnery and offers
Charlott to Valentine. Through Charlott's agency, Valentine tries to
elope with Floriante but Verole and his men intervene and carry off
the woman with whom he has left the nunnery. She, it turns out, is

Charlott, hoping to escape the nunnery through marriage. Ultimately the Count and Charlott are married, as are Valentine and Floriante.

In outline the indebtedness is clear and indeed Southerne has occasionally borrowed dialogue from the novel as well.[3] But there are a number of significant differences in tone and characterization. Behn's novel is a subdued variation on *Romeo and Juliet*, about neighboring young people who fall in love and suffer adversity; both are continually true to each other and chaste in their love. At the end the wounded Rinaldo, hearing that Count Vernole has married De Pais's daughter, undergoes the distress Romeo does over the false news of Juliet's death, but he is informed that the daughter is Charlott and reunited with Atlante for a happy ending. Southerne has given a more worldly cast to the story, infusing elements of Restoration comedy. Valentine is a man of the world whose feeling for Floriante is not all encompassing; after the first duel with Verole's bravos, he goes to bed with Lucia, who, as Sir Anthony Love, later helps Floriante escape. Moreover, Valentine and Floriante play a brief love-duel scene which identifies them nominally as the gay couple of the play. Finally, Southerne's Charlott appears in the disguise as part of a plot to trick Verole and effect Floriante's escape; Behn's Charlott hopes to marry Rinaldo, not Vernole, and her gaiety charms Vernole into accepting her when he realizes Atlante is lost. Although the reversal of alliances is abrupt in both, Behn's is far more developed.

Although the novel is clearly a major source, the characters are conventional and derivative. For example, the woman disguised as a man, familiar to us from Shakespeare's Viola and Rosalind, appears frequently in Restoration comedy, largely because actresses rather than boy actors now took the women's roles and male disguises made them more titillating to the audience; indeed, Southerne claimed in the dedicatory epistle that he had written the title role with Susannah Mountfort in mind and told the audience in the epilogue:

> You'll hear with Patience a dull scene, to see,
> In a contented lazy Waggery,
> The Female Montford bare above the knee. (258)

Previous Restoration comedies had exploited this audience delight in "breeches parts" by keeping the woman in disguise throughout the play.[4] By and large other roles are similarly anticipated during preceding decades, and the play draws heavily on convention without much specific borrowing.

If there is any particular influence on the play, it is the intrigue comedies of Aphra Behn, especially a play like *The Feign'd Curtizans* (1679), which more energetically presents similar disguises, confusions of identities and interests, threats of forced marriage and nunneries, a knightly gull, dashing Englishmen, and a foreign setting. In effect Southerne has adapted, expanded upon, and altered Behn's romantic novel *The Lucky Mistake* to meet the conventions of Behn's intrigue comedy. But, although the novel and a play like *The Feign'd Curtizans* are quite different in tone, one romantic and optimistic, the other skeptical and gay, both are far more consistent and uniform than Southerne's play; in *Sir Anthony Love*, as Hume makes clear, Southerne creates something of a "jumble" as he goes about "finding his bearings."[5]

II *"Sir Anthony Love"* and Sir Anthony Love

The tone of the play is decided largely by the title character. "Sir Anthony Love" is the male identity assumed by Lucia, a young Englishwoman who, having been "sold" by her aunt to Sir Gentle Golding, has robbed her keeper and fled England to follow in disguise her first love, Valentine, to Montpelier, the setting of the play. Early in the play she expresses hopes of winning him by her conduct as Sir Anthony; later, after granting him her favors disguised as a woman of Sir Anthony's acquaintance, she reveals her true identity and promises to help him procure Floriante. Shortly after, she allows Valentine to witness her gulling of Sir Gentle again. Finally, she aids Floriante's elopement by changing clothes with her and letting her run off with Valentine. Disguised as Floriante, she is married to Sir Gentle, who, horrified at his mistake, offers her a lucrative separate maintenance. Thus the action involving Valentine and Floriante is colored by the presence of Sir Anthony/Lucia at various points in the play—including the elopement scene where she kibitzes cynically about marriage—and also by the behavior of Valentine in relationship to both Sir Anthony and Lucia.

Sir Anthony Love is not only the title character; he/she is the pivotal presence in every action in the play but one (that involving Verole and Charlott). The other nominally romantic subplot is primarily a duel between Sir Anthony and the older, more reserved, more sober Ilford, another Englishman and Valentine's friend, for Volante, the sprightly ward of the Abbé. Continually Volante prefers Sir Anthony over Ilford, even when Ilford tries to explain to her that Sir Anthony has admitted he wants not marriage but sexual conquest. Ultimately Volante holds out for marriage and Sir Anthony obliges by letting Ilford, forced to concede Sir Anthony's ascendency, disguisé himself as a priest for the marriage and then take the mock-husband's place in bed. Ilford instead uses the occasion to shame her into a sense of her own folly and an appreciation of Ilford's love for her and regard for her, as well as a contempt for Sir Anthony's lack of regard for her. Thus, in a sense, this subplot undercuts Sir Anthony, but his/her continual and pervasive triumphing over both characters mitigates their effect.

Other, episodic elements of the play are equally dominated by Sir Anthony. Some involve a pilgrim whose mask of piety conceals a hypocritical villainy. Sir Anthony unveils him, but he forces Sir Gentle to exchange clothing with him, leading to comic confusion and Sir Gentle's apprehension as his own murderer. The whole business is a unit complete in a single act. Later the pilgrim (alternately called the palmer in the stage directions) lures Sir Anthony to a false assignation and attacks him, but is restrained by Valentine, whom Sir Anthony had brought along to enjoy the woman he supposes arranged the tryst. The pilgrim is in league with the Abbé, who has had Sir Anthony tricked so that the old man may attempt a homosexual seduction. He is horrified when Sir Anthony reveals her true identity. Here again the unit is self-contained in the play; when the whole action was cut from performance, it was not conspicuous by its absence.

The dual role of the title character reflects upon characters of either sex. As Sir Anthony, she is the stereotypical rakehell, the envy of all men, the delight of all women, combining bravado, vanity, and libertine skepticism of all relationships. Sir Anthony's sexual talk is more extravagant than that of Alberto, the rake of *The Disappointment*, and his success with women overshadows Valentine as the chief romantic male figure; indeed, twice in the play Sir Anthony provides women for Valentine—once the woman is herself, the second time it turns out to be the Abbé, a curious alternation of male-female reversals. In either case Valentine is being provided for sexually, as Sir Anthony has previously provided for him financially. Later he/she even makes feasible his marriage to Floriante. Throughout, Valentine is an ardent admirer of Sir Anthony; indeed, all the men acknowledge Sir Anthony's superiority in one way or another: the pilgrim by thinking him a more errant Villain, the Abbé by doting on his perfectly desirable boyish charms, and both of them, together with Sir Gentle, by being continually outwitted by him.

Sir Anthony even dominates the delineation of Ilford, a man of some reserve and sense who continually finds Sir Anthony's extravagance at best imprudent and at worst perverse, chiding him for unnecessary violence and disapproving of his indiscretion. In the battles of wit Ilford is continually bested; in the competition for Volante he is constantly runner-up and ultimately must capitulate to Sir Anthony for the opportunity to win Volante himself. Thus, as the play's "man of discretion," comparable in some ways to Lorenzo in *The Disappointment* (though Jordan sees him derived from aspects of Vernole in *The Lucky Mistake*), Ilford is seldom able to rise above the moments when he is shown to be foolish or inferior.

The strength of the title character in her female identity affects the standing of the other women in the play. As Lucia, she is the clear-headed fallen woman, amoral, practical, and sentimental: she cheats her keeper again and again, grants her favors to Valentine before and during the play, and, completely accepting the double standard, refuses to marry Valentine and helps him win Floriante. Her vivacity, wit, and independence make the gaiety and charm of the sisters, in those few scenes where they are displayed, seem slight by comparison; and Floriante's moment of coyness about marriage, in the brief love-duel with Valentine, is undercut by Sir Anthony/Lucia's presence as Valentine's recently enjoyed ex-lover—her constant interjections cynically misdirect Floriante's gay sententiae. In consequence, Floriante's decision to marry Valentine—"since Marriage at best is a venture, I had as good make it my self, as let another make it for me, at my Cost" (250)—seems ambiguous; her character is so underdeveloped in comparison with Lucia's—we do not know her well enough to know for certain such remarks are merely a playful disguising of sincere feelings, as it is so often in earlier plays—and the surface skepticism of such a remark echoes less forcibly the recurring antimatrimonialism of Sir Anthony/Lucia.

By comparison Volante's sprightliness seems to be more giddy than gay—ultimately she is chastened and embarrassed. Charlott, noted for her gaiety throughout Behn's novel, is made more calculating here by the abbreviation of her role. Her last word on

her union with Count Verole comes before his abrupt announce-
ment of his good fortune in gaining Charlott, after he has lost
Floriante and been gulled by Lucia. Charlott explains in Act V that
she is "not so much in love with the Count, as I am out of love with
a Nunnery: Any Man had been as well-come" (249).[6] Neither of
these women says anything on their final reappearance on stage to
lead us to believe the circumstances of their unions are other than
equivocal; in fact, the play ends with its focus upon the marriage of
Sir Gentle and Lucia, on a note of celebration over her final
triumph in the play.

III Critical Responses to Sir Anthony Love

Sir Anthony/Lucia triumphs continually; she is never defeated
and her views are never repudiated by the context of the play.
Because she is so triumphant and so representative of the free
gallantry condoned, if not celebrated, in earlier Restoration comedy, critics have constantly seen the play as undeviatingly in the
camp of what Hume calls "hard comedy"—plays "cutting, cynical,
and libertine." Dodds claimed that "Southerne's comic philosophy
in this play is entirely within the artificial convention of the comedy
of manners,"[7] and Nicoll called it "a fair specimen of mannerised
comedy."[8] Schneider has gone so far as to pronounce that through
the character of Sir Anthony Love/Lucia "Thomas Southerne
furthers the doctrine that plain-dealing whoredom has much to be
said for it."[9] But none of these comments takes into consideration
the fact that, while Southerne may be observing the form of libertine intrigue comedy, the tone of the play is far closer to the gloomy
comedies of Otway than the lively comedies of Behn. Though not so
dark, so cynical, so close to bordering on a disgust for the very
milieu it represents as Otway's plays do, *Sir Anthony Love* is clouded by a similar darkness in the presentation of character, a similar
lack of sympathy with the folly of the play's society.

A clear example of the relationship between Otway and
Southerne in this play lies in the depiction of the Abbé and his
notorious seduction scene. Initially the Abbé is a cheerful proponent
of the interest of the lovers, a figure in opposition to the "Spanish
strictness" of his brother, Count Canaille, like Sir Jocelyn Jolly in
Etherege's *She Would If She Could*. But he is also a religious figure
whose casual disregard for the solemnity of his office indicates an
underlying hypocrisy that the seduction scene makes manifest. He

resembles no other character in Restoration comedy more closely than Otway's Sir Jolly Jumble, the panderer in the *The Soldier's Fortune* who can't keep his hands off the hero and who asks, as his reward for arranging an assignation, to be allowed to watch the consummation. Moreover, the Abbé's homosexuality is not simply part of his characterization, as it is with Jumble, but the object of a scene expressly designed to make it explicit to the audience. It is the play's most potent satirical moment, one which continually raises difficulties among critics.

In performance the scene was cut because, according to the Epistle Dedicatory, Southerne did not want to "run the venture of offending the Women; not that there is one indecent Expression in it; but the over-fine Folk might run it into a Design I never had in my Head: My Meaning was, to expose the Vice; and I thought it could not be more contemptibly expos'd, than in the Person of a Wanton old Man, that must make ev'n the most reasonable Pleasure ridiculous." Nothing in Southerne's previous or subsequent work can lead us to doubt that he was indeed satirizing homosexuality, rather than promoting the bisexuality G. Wilson Knight sees recurrent in Restoration comedy[10] or, in Dodds's phrase, making "an unsavory attempt . . . to pander to the most depraved tastes of his audience."[11] In fact, Montague Summers has argued the reverse, that the scene was cut because "it was thought to reflect far too openly upon the homosexuality of William of Orange, whose tastes in that direction were being pretty freely glanced at in contemporary lampoon and pasquinado."[12] Summers's statement should be viewed with caution—a general hit at homosexuality is not necessarily a direct hit at the king, whose inclinations in that area are still a topic of debate—and we should beware the attractive lure of mere topical allusion. On either side we may have the arguments of "over-fine folk running it into a design Southerne never had in his head." However, although there is nothing expressly topical in the scene, it is clearly satirical and the satirical perspective is far more important to the play than has been generally allowed.

Kenneth Muir has suggested that " 'Sir Anthony' is used by Southerne to satirize the behavior of the gallants of the period,"[13] and his remark is a clue to the organizing principle behind the play. We should suspect Southerne's satiric intent not simply from the scene with the Abbé or the portrait of a rakehell Lucia gives us, but also from the continual failure of the other characters to live up to the norms of their conventions. All the characters usually the chief personages of Restoration comedy are here stereotypes *manqués*, forever overshadowed by the exuberant stereotype supreme, the role of Sir Anthony Love as Lucia creates it. In this sense *Sir Anthony Love* subtly is satirizing the deficiencies of the conventional characters of Restoration comedy. Certainly nothing in Southerne's previous plays should lead us to expect a play condoning free-gallantry. We need only consider the treatment of Alberto and the sympathy with Erminia, Angelline, and particularly Juliana, Alberto's cast mistress, in *The Disappointment* to see where Southerne's sympathies lay in the past. And nothing in the plays which follow contradicts this view. In their own ways the two great comedies to come are also directed at the deficiencies of Restoration stage conventions and the social deficiencies they reflect.

Yet, however accurate this interpretation of the play's organizing principle may be, a few qualifications must be included. One is that the play is uncharacteristic of Southerne in important ways. Most significantly, it lacks clear sympathy with any of its characters, and sympathy is one of Southerne's most central concerns. In a play by Behn, a woman ruined as Lucia has been would get her revenge by marriage and adultery; in *The Disappointment* Southerne shows his sympathy with the fallen woman by placing her on a par with the chaste women of the play in the finale. But that sympathy does not carry over into this play. A whole psychology of the fallen woman that one might expect is absent here.

A second qualification is more central to the final evaluation of this play. We must recall that the sharpest satire of the play was never presented on stage and that what remained without it and without clear indications of sympathy with any characters is rather equivocal and open for interpretation. While Southerne seems indeed to be struggling to "find his bearings" in this play, he provides insufficient bearings for his audience. Perhaps the widely attested success of the play was due indeed to the acting of Susannah Mountfort, but partly as well it was due to the fact that the use of conventional characters and the lack of any clear reaction against them in the play allowed the audiences the opportunity to respond to the play as they wished rather than as the playwright might have had them. Thus the strength of the play carried it and the weaknesses were not clearly understood by the audiences as weaknesses.

Most critics, even those who ultimately do not value the play highly, have seen some reasons for its success. Dodds believed it "the best of our author's three comedies in the manners style";[14] he felt it was a success because Southerne here "depended upon a genius for evolving situations rich in comic power."[15] Summers called it "replete with spirit, sparkle, and abandon, and equal to the raciest scenes of Vanbrugh and Farquhar themselves";[16] Muir allowed that it "has some lively scenes, some good comic situations, and some amusing dialogue";[17] Hume writes that the plot "is dazzlingly energetic; lusty and vivacious action combines with a fine display of wit."[18] But most have also observed that the play is overlong, too farcical for modern tastes, and often strained by "over-clever wit" or marred by Southerne's prevailing weakness—"the over-use of theatrical broken sentences, wherein the meaning of one speaker is continued or perverted by another."[19] Southerne's first attempt at comedy may well be often uneven, the wit often forced, but nonetheless it was to be more successful on the stage than his next two, both of which were theatrical failures and Southerne's masterworks.

CHAPTER 4

The Wives Excuse

I *Background*

*T*HE *Wives Excuse, or, Cuckolds Make Themselves* met a dismal reception from its original audience. Premiering in December 1691, it failed immediately, and so far as we know did not play beyond its initial performance. It was entered for publication in the Term Catalogues for February 1692 and appeared with commendatory verses by Dryden and a defense of the play in Southerne's dedicatory epistle to Thomas Wharton. The fact of its stage failure, despite a brilliant cast headed by Betterton as Lovemore, Kynaston as Wellvile, Elizabeth Barry as Mrs. Friendall, Anne Bracegirdle as Mrs. Sightly, and Susannah Mountfort as Mrs. Witwoud, has long guided critics to neglect the play or dismiss it as simply another manners comedy; but in some circles in its own time the play was admired, and in recent years scholars have come to appreciate it more fully.

Unlike *Sir Anthony Love*, there is nothing equivocal about *The Wives Excuse*. Every element in the play contributes to a central purpose, an attack on free-gallantry. The main plot involves the attempts of the rake Lovemore to seduce Mrs. Friendall, the wife of a foolish and unsuccessful philanderer. Initially Lovemore hopes to drive the wife from the husband by exposing him as a coward, but he is thwarted first by her public attempt to keep her husband from fighting Ruffle, the thug whom Lovemore has hired to insult him, and then by her arranging to frighten Ruffle into a public apology. Nonetheless, Lovemore, certain that Friendall's face-saving has been engineered by his wife, hopes that he has succeeded in her mind, if not in public, and pretends to have helped her keep her secret. When, at a masquerade, the whole company discovers Friendall in the arms of another woman, Mrs. Witwoud, and husband and wife separate, Lovemore voices optimism over an eventual conquest.

At the same time another plot involves another set of machinations for seduction. Mrs. Witwoud, to keep her seduced niece, Fanny, from public exposure, persuades her seducer, Wilding, to drop her in favor of Mrs. Sightly, Mrs. Witwoud's high-principled friend. Wilding's attempt to know Mrs. Sightly alarms Wellvile, who has never attempted her in the years of their acquaintance, and also undermines his faith in her integrity—he begins to believe she is in the market for a lover and offers himself in Wilding's stead, immediately alienating her. Mrs. Sightly rejects Mrs. Witwoud for plotting against her character and Witwoud in turn plots revenge by disguising herself as Mrs. Sightly and allowing herself to be seduced by Wilding. But plans backfire: Friendall, who has been pursuing Sightly also, is sent in place of Wilding, leading to the exposure which climaxes the main plot. In the secondary plot Mrs. Witwoud is disgraced, Fanny is reported to have run away, and Mrs. Sightly views Wellvile's contrite proposal of marriage with caution.

In his edition of the play Ralph Thornton, while suggesting a number of possible sources for various bits of action, including plays by Behn, Otway, Shadwell, and Molière, acknowledges that such indebtedness is vague and "more in the spirit of the hearty comedy of intrigue than in specific borrowings."[1] Southerne, drawing carefully upon Restoration stage conventions in the play, in effect uses them to subvert the tradition. The triangle plot is a staple of Restoration comedy, but here Southerne rings changes on the two directions the plot has taken. In Shadwell, Otway, and Behn, for example, triangle plots lead to cuckolding intrigues—an unfaithful wife punishes a foolish or philandering husband by submitting to a lover.[2] The corollary to this is the triangle plot of reforming comedy, carried over from the moralistic comedies of Brome and Shirley in the 1630s, and only intermittently offered on the Restoration stage, as in D'Urfey's *The Virtuous Wife*, where a virtuous wife resists the blandishments of a rake, reforms him by her exemplary behavior, and wins her errant husband to sense. Underlying the libertine comedy is the assumption that arranged marriages inevitably fail and can only be made palatable by infidelity; the assumption behind the exemplary comedy is that marriage is a sacrament which may not be violated, particularly by a woman, no matter what the provocation, and that inevitably it will be made acceptable if the wife maintains her honor. In either case the actions of plays upholding these views, when they have a viewpoint at all, are structured to prove them.

II *Southerne and "The Whole Business of Cuckolding"*

In *The Wives Excuse* Southerne "puts the whole business of cockolding on a psychological basis; he is more interested in accounting for it than in demonstrating it for the delight of the pit and the boxes."[3] Consequently he merges the two traditions, in effect taking from each what is true to the social situation and the psychology of the participants, and eschewing in either what is didactically unsupported or unmotivated and formulaic. He attempts, moreover, to make his alterations clear by an unusual device, the discussion of the play itself in the middle of its performance.[4] Provoked by Friendall, whom he knows has made advances to Mrs. Sightly, Wellvile mocks him to his face by explaining to him a play he claims he is writing:

Well. You must know then, Sir, I am scandaliz'd extreamly to see the Women upon the Stage make Cuckolds at that insatiable Rate they do in all our modern Comedies: Without any other Reason from the Poets, but, because a Man is married he must be a Cuckold: Now, Sir, I think, the Women are most unconscionably injur'd by this general Scandal upon their Sex; therefore to do 'em what Service I can in their Vindication, I design to write a Play, and call it—
Mr. Fri. Ay, what, I beseech you, I love to know the Name of a new Play.
Well. The Wives Excuse: Or, Cuckolds Make Themselves.

When Friendall asks for the characters, Wellvile gives him his own:

Why I design to shew a fine young Woman marry'd to an impertinent, nonsensical, silly, intrigueing, cowardly, good-for-nothing Coxcomb.

Friendall insists that the husband be made a cuckold, "for such a Character, Gentlemen, will vindicate a Wife in any thing she can do to him." Wellvile replies that he is "satisfied he ought to be a Cuckold"; however, the question of the wife alters his willingness to make him one.

Well. I have not yet determined how to dispose of her. But in regard to the Ladies, I believe I shall make her Honest at last.

Mr. Fri. I think the Ladies ought to take it very ill of you, if you do: But if she proves Honest to the last, that's certain, 'tis more than the Fellow deserves.

(V. I, pp. 314 - 15)

In this interchange Friendall, the foolish husband of the play, upholds the traditional view that the wives' excuse for adultery is the folly of their husbands, a viewpoint repeatedly expressed in the play. Such a view is not without its shading of interpretation, however. In *Sir Anthony Love* the palmer cynically says,

> Men are to blame, who like young Conjurers, prove
> (Safe in the Circle of a Wedding-Ring)
> The Magick Spell of Wedlock upon Love:
> So, Cuckolds make themselves by Marrying.

(228)

In his view the very act of marriage guarantees the loss of love and the inevitability of infidelity. But such is not the view of *The Wives Excuse* or of any of its characters. Here, cuckolds make themselves not simply by marrying—which implies a universal inevitability—but by their actions outside of their marriages—which indicates individual responsibility. The husband is at fault, not the institution of marriage per se or, as is specifically made clear in this play, the wife. Southerne, through Wellvile here and throughout the play, speculates on the effect of a husband's folly upon a wife, treating cuckolding as a punishment that society may see as fitting for the husband but which is nonetheless an action that brings the wife no credit. In fact, to uphold cuckolding as a permissible alternative is to view the wife completely as an adjunct to the husband, reinforcing his honor, punishing his dishonor, without a separate integrity of her own.

Really the play is about the effect of the mores of a society upon the conduct of individuals within it. Southerne makes clear the mores of this society by introducing a unique opening scene. Where, conventionally, Restoration comedy opens with the principal characters at conversation, explaining their plots and delineating their own characters and those of offstage characters, or else leaps into the action which motivates the plot, *The Wives Excuse* opens with a gathering of servants of the principal characters, offering insights into their masters, setting the tone of cynicism and opportunism in the play, and establishing the milieu. The servants reflect either the attitudes of their masters—as Wilding's servant is the most rakish and unfeeling—or the values of society at large—like the Friendalls' servant, willing to be paid for his cunning and discretion by both the philandering husband and his mistress's potential lovers. All the conversation is about the pursuit of women. The Friendalls' servant's willingness to help husband and horner for a fee reflects the calculating callousness of this world, as does Wilding's footman's expression of the prevailing assumption about married women: "Every Man has hopes of a new marry'd Woman: For she marries to like her Man and if upon Trial she finds she can't like her Husband, she'll find some body else that she can like, in a very little time, I warrant her, or change her Men 'till she does" (271). The negotiations between the footmen of Wilding, Lovemore, and Friendall preview the cold merchandising of women which goes on throughout the play.

The characters are divided as to sex by nature but into other roles according to the prescriptions of the society toward the sexes. Thus the men are uniformly predators and the women uniformly prey, and the dominant theme of the play is the victimization by men of women according to the conventions of the stage and the traditions of the society.

III *"The Hard Condition of a Woman's Fate"*

Mrs. Friendall, the principal example of the "hard condition of a woman's fate," is the figure most fully realized in the play. She is a complex character, a woman married by arrangement who is unwilling to become either of the Restoration's stereotypes of the Wife. To begin with, she is fully cognizant of her own identity. After three months of marriage and after her husband has already turned to pursuit of other women, including his wife's best friend, Mrs. Sightly, Mrs. Friendall explains to her that " 'tis with the tenderest Concern for my own Reputation, that I see my Husband daily trifle away his so notoriously, in one Folly or other of the Town"(282). She is willing to be the dutiful wife, but only to a husband who merits it, for she observes, "How despicable a Condition must that Matrimony be, when the Husband (whom we look upon as a Sanctuary for a Woman's Honour) must be obliged to the Discretion and Management of a Wife, for the Security of his Own!"(293). Nonetheless, despite her full awareness of Friendall's faults, she refuses to become the wanton wife of Restoration comedy, because she has too strong a sense of her own worth, apart from her husband's. She tells Lovemore that "I won't justifie his Faults, but because he does not take that care of me he shou'd, must not I have that regard to my self I ought? What I do is for my own sake"(322). Continually she reacts as one who must be aware of her own interest as well as that of her husband. Thus she responds neither to the temptations of a lover, which would disgrace her in her own eyes, nor unthinkingly to the sanctity of her marriage vow, which would make her a fool.

The high point of the psychological development of Mrs. Friendall's character comes in scenes between her and Lovemore, particularly the scene in Act V when she admits his attraction for her. By relenting in her harsh judgment of him, she condemns the society at large and elucidates the dilemma of a woman trapped in a distasteful marriage:

Nay, I don't blame you for designing upon me, Custom has fashion'd it into the way of living among the Men; and you may be i'th' right to all the Town: But let me be i'th' right too to my Sex and to my self: Thus far may be excus'd: You've prov'd your Passion, and my Virtue try'd; but all beyond that Tryal is my Crime, and not to be forgiven: Therefore I intreat you, don't make it impossible to me for the future, to receive you as a Friend; for I must own, I would secure you always for my Friend: Nay more, I will confess my Heart to you: If I could make you mine— . . . But I am marry'd, only pity me—

(338)

The town *has* repeatedly offered her the wives' excuse, expressed sympathy with the wife of such a fool, and, at least implicitly but more often explicitly, encouraged her to punish him with horns. But she has seen what they have not, that to do so is not to be "in the right" to her sex or herself. Yet, in spite of her ability to resist Lovemore in a scene Smith calls "an outstanding example in the drama of the period of a virtuous woman resisting a seducer entirely without heroics,"[5] she is no exemplary stick figure—despite everything she knows about Lovemore, she is attracted to him. Muir has observed that "it is rare for a dramatist to deal with such a situation in a cool and sensible way, without righteous indignation on the part of the woman and without the attempted use of force by the man." He goes on to say that "the woman's confession that she finds the man attractive and his proposal a compliment is psychologically truer than many of the reactions ascribed to virtuous wives by dramatists of the period; and it is quite different in tone from similar scenes written by writers of sentimental comedy."[6]

It is important here to realize that once she has left the stage Lovemore responds to her request for compassion with disdain, noting in soliloquy that the fact of her marriage, her inability to encumber him after an affair, was a primary factor in being attracted to her to begin with. Thus at the end of the play we have a fully developed picture of the options open to Mrs. Friendall when she separates from her husband. She tells him, "The unjust World, let what will be the Cause of our Complaint (as there is Cause sufficient still at home) condemn us to a Slavery for Life: and if by Separation we get free, then all our Husband's Faults are laid on us: This hard Condition of a Woman's Fate, I've often weigh'd, therefore resolv'd to bear: And I have born; O! what have I not born?" (345). But although she is free from her husband's presence, and given a separate maintenance, she is still his wife and her options are still the same as they were before: a willing blindness to his folly and dutiful silence; indifference to her own ideas of morality and acceptance of a lover (or, inevitably, a series of lovers); or life with neither husband nor lover, unless the husband's death should free her to marry again. The hard condition of a woman's fate is the distastefulness of her options under the arranged marriage, an element of her society which leaves little room for the happiness of individuals.

Although Mrs. Friendall is the most fully developed character to feel the weight of the social inequities, all the women feel them to some degree. Mrs. Sightly is made the object of others' machinations, her character called into question completely without her knowing, even by Wellvile, the man who most should know her. Although she has too much strength of character to be a victim of the plots of Mrs. Witwoud and Wilding, she nonetheless is tainted by them and, but for the discovery of Mrs. Witwoud's final plot, might have been dishonored. Fanny, Mrs. Witwoud's cousin, the victim whom Mrs. Sightly is to replace, is not only deflowered in the course of the play but made a public scandal by running away, as Wilding has encouraged her, from an arranged marriage. Wilding claims that by seducing her he has merely been "teaching her a very good Trade," and certainly Fanny, by the public knowledge of her seduction, has had her options in this society limited. Even Mrs. Witwoud, who seems to be the tool of the men and the enemy of the women, is a victim of society's double stan-

dards. Her gossip either reports on the moral decadence she
believes pervasive in her milieu or reveals by its falsity her own
sense of malice—and occasionally it does both. Yet there are hints
by Mrs. Teazall and Mrs. Sightly that Mrs. Witwoud has had an il-
licit relationship with a married man, that she is "notoriously abandon'd to the Beastly Love of a Fellow, that no Body else can look
upon" (329), and her resentment is continually fueled by her inability to inspire the men to the same desire that the women of virtue do. In the end she leaves the stage disgraced, followed by
Springame, who is eager to take advantage of her new accessibility.

At the end of the play only Mrs. Sightly faces a future over which
we can feel any optimism at all. That of Mrs. Witwoud is particularly bleak, but so is Fanny's; and Mrs. Friendall's is completely
problematic. Smith believes that we are to think it "unlikely that
Lovemore will have to wait long for his triumph, which will then set
him free for other game,"⁷ but I rather think Southerne intends the
ending to be ambiguous in that regard, to make the audience have
to think about her alternatives rather than lament or cheer the inevitable.

IV   The Varieties of Predator

For the men, on the other hand, very little has changed.
Lovemore's hopes are improved, Friendall's opportunities to pursue
his pleasures are more unrestrained. For Wilding, Courtall, and
Springame, nothing has changed at all. Only Wellvile shows any
signs of having learned anything from the experience of the play,
but even he shares most of the instincts of the male portion of this
society.

All the men are defined in terms of predation. Minor characters
are named for their interests in seduction: Courtall thinks the "enjoyment the dull part of an intrigue" and never takes advantage of
his success; Springame is far more interested in the consummation
of an affair rather than the seduction and, as Mrs. Witwoud complains, "comes so quick upon that Business, he won't afford a
Woman a reasonable liking-time, to make a decent Excuse to her
self, if she shou'd allow him a Favour" (278). Both men comple-
ment one another; in a similar way so do Lovemore and Wilding.

Wilding is the most dangerous predator of the lot, because so
many of his predations are motivated by malice and egoism. He is
unfeeling enough to jest with his servant about the deflowered Fan-

ny; and when the servant asks him why he took pains to persuade her to run away from her aunt "when I know you never design to take care of her your self," he replies, "the best Reason I know of, is, (besides the Reputation of undoing her): it looks kind, at the time, to talk of providing for the Woman that does one the Favour. 'Twas a very plausible Argument, to cozen her into a Consent; level to my Design of Lying with her, and carry'd to the very Mark of Love" (295). Wilding uses the psychology of young girls to "cozen" them, the entire relationship turning on the importance of his succeeding at any cost and of having a reputation for success, since that enhances his standing among the men and lures on other young girls who are naive enough to think they can reform him. Thus it is Wilding Mrs. Witwoud hopes to succumb to in disguise as Mrs. Sightly, since she is sure Wilding will broadcast his conquest. His calculating sexual Machiavellianism, his indifference to the fate of Fanny, his inability to avoid pursuit even when he has given his word, all make him a particularly unattractive example of the rake rampant.

Lovemore has considerably more discretion and equal cunning. He too works on the psychology of his victim; as Mrs. Friendall observes of him, he has "proceeded like a Man of Experience in this Business, and taken the natural Road to undermine most Women," improving upon Friendall's weaknesses "as much as they could bear upon the Conduct of his Wife" (338). His awareness that he may have succeeded in separating husband and wife in her mind, even if he has failed in the public eye, is an astute observation. But however subtle and discreet he may appear, he is nonetheless as callous as Wilding, and exceeds him only in caution, as befits a man whose prey is principally married women, not naive virgins. After Mrs. Friendall reveals most fully her potential vulnerability, he displays to the audience the full shallowness of his feeling for her:

Pity her! She does not deserve it, that won't better her Condition when she may: But she's marry'd, she says; why, that was the best of my Reasons of following her at first; and I like her so well, as she's another Man's Wife, I should hardly mend the matter by making her my own. I won't think yet my two Months thrown away upon her: One time or other, some way or other, I may be the better for her. (339)

Surely this example of what Kaufman calls "Lovemore's chop-licking Machiavellianism" cannot make an audience sanguine

about Mrs. Friendall's future should she submit to him. Lovemore
is not the attractive gallant so often offered as an alternative to the
foolish husband in earlier cuckolding intrigues, nor is there any
likelihood of his reformation, as in the exemplary comedies.

Neither is Friendall quite the husband of earlier traditions. He is
foolish, cowardly, and vain, but he is not a disgusting old man and
the scene in which he is insulted by Ruffle portrays him more as a
victim than a butt. In the end, at the separation, he is not a sputter-
ing dupe, but a reasonable and well-spoken man eager to take his
place among the gallants. Except for his lack of success we have no
reason not to place him among them: certainly his response to the
cuckolding of the wife in Wellvile's play demonstrates that his iden-
tifications are wholly with the gallants, not the husbands, of the
world. Moreover, Friendall is not the good-hearted husband led
astray, either, the man worthy of the patient and long-suffering wife
who brings him to his senses. With Friendall, as with the other
members of this traditional triangle, Southerne has wrought
changes that make his depiction more real, less contrived, more disturbing. In his view the wife's alternatives are between different
manifestations of essentially the same mentality.

Even Wellvile, the author-surrogate of the play, suffers from the
malaise of the society. Like Lorenzo, his prototype in *The Disappointment*, Wellvile is the man of reason and honor—his long
relationship with Mrs. Sightly has been respectable all the way.
Like Ilford, the man of discretion of *Sir Anthony Love*, Wellvile is
not infallible, and his belief that as an old admirer, he stands "as
fair, and have as good a Title to put in my Claim" to Mrs. Sightly as
Wilding, demonstrates how infectious the daily round of manipula-
tion and seduction has become. Mrs. Sightly is outraged at both his
willingness to believe her in the market for a lover and his insensitivity in describing an affair with her in terms of the marketplace.
In the end he is as much a part of the destruction of Friendall's
marriage, by his desire to punish Friendall for courting Mrs. Sightly, as Wilding or Lovemore; but he is the only male who offers a
woman an honorable alternative. Mrs. Sightly's temporary refusal
of his proposal of marriage, while suggesting the probability of an
acceptance some time in the future, depicts not only her continuing
resentment but her caution in trusting his judgment as fully as she
once did. In other words, the only relationship in the play between
honorable, respectable, sincere people has been tainted and tar-
nished by the mores of the milieu in which they live.

V   *The Play and Its Critics*

The close identification of Wellvile with Southerne himself gives
us, as Hume notes, "a strong sense of the author's unhappy entrap-
ment in a degraded society."[8] Except in the virtue of Mrs. Friendall
and Mrs. Sightly, neither of whom exhibits perfect judgment, there
is no positive force in the play; it is instead consistently disturbing
throughout, and unquestionably this consistency worked against the
play's commercial success. His audience, Sutherland concludes,
"did not want to have their favorite comic theme subjected to such
an analysis, however penetrating; for this was to spoil their fun, to
question the very assumptions on which the comedy of sex rested."[9]
Southerne himself pointed out, in his dedication, that his critics
were "affronted at Mrs. *Friendall*: For those Sparks who were most
offended with her Virtue in Publick, are the Men who lose little by
it in Private; and if all the Wives in Town were of her Mind, those
metled Gentlemen wou'd be found to have the least to do, in making 'em otherwise." Southerne's subversion of the conventions won
him little support from the average playgoer, who depended so
much upon the predictability of convention for his entertainment.
Southerne demonstrates his awareness of the problem in his motto
affixed to the published edition: *Nihil est his, qui placere volunt,
tam adversarium, quam expectatio* (Nothing is to them, who wish to
please, so adverse as expectation).[10] The expectations of the
audience essentially stifled innovation or individual execution of the
conventions.[11]

Curiously enough this same problem of expectation among
scholar-critics has hampered an appreciation of the play's ex-
cellence. Nicoll classified the play as "mannerised comedy of the
same class as *Sir Anthony Love*"—to which it has little
resemblance—and dismissed it as "not a very good play."[12] Dodds,
as we might expect, was utterly repelled, saying that "a drearier
round of cuckolding and wenching would be hard to find" and
labeling it a "typical comedy of manners" with a "dull series of
stereotyped intrigues," concluding, "Our study of the comedy,
therefore, must be a study in mediocrity."[13] For him the play's only
virtue is that it contains in Mrs. Friendall a prototype of the sentimental heroine, although, as Kaufman points out, she is above
that stereotype as well.[14] Only slowly have such views as those of
Nicoll and Dodds been overshadowed by beliefs in the play's power
and intelligence.

The beginnings of such an evaluation are present with the play's publication, however, Motteux in the *Gentleman's Journal* urging that "it will bear a Reading; which some that meet with a better Fate too often do not,"[15] and Dryden assuring Southerne in the commendatory verses that "the Readers will be thine," and comparing him to Terence: "Like him thy Thoughts are Pure, thy Language clean, /Ev'n Lewdness is made Moral, in thy Scene." Contemporary critics have come to agree with the justice of these remarks, and perhaps to value it more highly. Smith said he would "rate *The Wives Excuse* one of the five most considerable comedies written between 1660 and 1700";[16] he felt that in Southerne's "ability to fathom and judge human nature Congreve himself surpasses *The Wives Excuse* only in his own masterpiece."[17] Hume calls it "a brilliant play" and notes that "only Otway and Wycherley, among Southerne's predecessors, had produced anything like so angry, ugly, and effective a satire."[18] Kenneth Muir, in *The Comedy of Manners*, accorded Southerne a chapter, equal rank with Congreve and Vanbrugh. A. H. Scouten has asserted the play's place as a pivotal one in the development of the comedy of manners in the 1690s: "If this play goes unread or passes unnoticed, the historian is more likely to see only the works of Congreve and not observe the cluster of similar plays. . . . Furthermore, if the play were examined, students of Restoration drama would have seen that it contains one of the main characteristics which distinguish the comedies of this later period from those between 1668 to 1676, the shift from unmarried 'gay couples' to the problems of a married couple."[19] Scouten goes on to trace the theme of marriage through the comedies of Vanbrugh and Congreve to *The Beaux' Stratagem* of Farquhar, in fact through the three writers most often anthologized and studied as the best playwrights and most important representatives of their age.[20] In summary, *The Wives Excuse* is not only powerful and brilliant in its own right, but highly significant as the starting place for a small group of plays which include among them the very best of Restoration comedy.

CHAPTER 5

The Maid's Last Prayer

I *Southerne's Wycherleyan Satire*

THE premiere of *the Maid's Last Prayer, or, Any Rather Than Fail*, with Mrs. Barry as Lady Malepert, Mrs. Bracegirdle as Lady Trickitt, and Susannah Mountfort as Lady Susan, including a song by Congreve and music set by Henry Purcell, was followed by its publication two weeks later. The *Gentleman's Journal*, dated January 1692/3 but issued in March, mentions its third and fourth performances; the *London Gazette* for March 9 - 13 informs us of the play's publication on the thirteenth. Like Southerne's previous play, it did not last long on the stage.

In the commendatory verses to *The Wives Excuse*, Dryden had advised Southerne:

> But if thou wou'dst be seen, as well as read;
> Copy one living Author, and one dead;
> The Standard of the Style, let Etherege be:
> For Wit, th' Immortal Spring of Wycherley.
> Learn after both, to draw some just Design,
> And the next Age will learn to copy thine.

Southerne may have taken his advice seriously, for certainly there is a greater range of event in this play; and no other play of the period so completely matches the vigor and bite of Wycherley's satires as this. The exposure of the social undersurface of the lives of fashionable women recalls *The Country Wife* and the characters of Granger and Gayman echo the forthright Manly and libertine Freeman of *The Plain Dealer*; Granger, like Manly, seeks a sexual punishment of an errant woman. The negatively powerful comedies of Otway may have contributed as well, but the chief influence is unquestionably Wycherley. Muir has made an important distinction between them, however: "Wycherley depicts a society of cuckolds

65

and cuckold makers, or promiscuity under a veil of hypocrisy, but the women, corrupt as they are, seek only sexual pleasure. In Southerne's plays, and particularly in *The Maid's Last Prayer*, the women are more mercenary."[1] Such a shift in emphasis alters the way the audience perceives the events of a play and the audience for this play was dismayed by what it saw; as Hume suggests, "this was comedy too hard-bitten for the mid-nineties."[2]

In *The Maid's Last Prayer* Southerne not only revives the manner of Wycherley, but actually extends it; for he "uses the 'free-gallantry' pattern not merely to attack immorality and hypocrisy in women and folly in husbands, but to judge and condemn free-gallantry itself."[3] A good many plays of the Restoration best known for their antimatrimonial wit and sexual intrigue only nominally advocate free gallantry, since they end, usually, in marriages between compatible lovers. Here Southerne in effect exercises the comedy of sex in all its abandon in order to devastate it. As in *The Wives Excuse* the conventional actions are undercut by the examination of motive. With the possible exception of Maria, a character of charm, sense, and affability left rather undeveloped in the play, no one operates out of generous or unselfish motives. The unfaithful wives are motivated by mercenary rather than sexual desires; the predatory role is taken by women here and the three rakes, Granger, Gayman, and Garnish, all suffer humiliation and dissatisfaction at the hands of women who have accepted the marital and sexual premises of their society and capitalized upon them. In a sense Southerne fulfills the expectations raised by these conventional characters without allowing the audience to enjoy that fulfillment. Deliberately he attempts to sour their taste for the libertine ethic and turn them away from its most characteristic expression, the sexual intrigue. Whatever else the complicated motives of those who seek marriage in Act Five may be, they are as much mutual expressions of a desire to leave this society. However equivocal these unions may seem, they are positive by comparison with the unions the play has already explored.

As he had in *The Disappointment* and in *The Wives' Excuse*, Southerne here gives us a panoply of comparisons, characterizations whose motives echo and reverberate off one another throughout the play. But he is not so able to keep them parallel and significantly related; two minor actions, including the title plot, tend to seem separate and extraneous, as if Southerne had simply attempted to include too much. In that way the few weaknesses of *The Maid's*

Last Prayer resemble those of *Sir Anthony Love*, but the miniatures he paints of separate characters in soliloquy or in brief revealing exchanges of dialogue are a marked advance in his control of psychology. No longer is his portraiture done in flamboyant imitations of Shakespeare, but rather in more realistic dramatic moments more appropriate to the context of the play.

II   The Free-Gallantry Ethic and the Play's Women

The women of *The Maid's Last Prayer* are unusual in Southerne's canon because they are generally either promiscuous or malicious. His earlier portraits of "fallen women" are nowhere near as harsh: Juliana is true to the man who betrayed her and is essentially a good woman wronged; Lucia chooses only Valentine, her first love, for her bed partner during the play and seems justified in her trickery of her keeper, but her behavior is more high-spirited and skeptical than anything else. Here, however, the chief female characters are involved in one way or another with the acquisition of wealth through cold-blooded sex; promiscuity and malice infect all their actions; yet even here Southerne is able to create sympathy for them, even if only partially, by his thorough exploration of their characters.

The life that Lady Trickitt leads is so independent of her husband that he never appears in the play—at best he is a barely relevant off-stage presence. Lady Trickitt's life is completely centered upon her self. Her primary passion is money, and the means by which she acquires it are indifferent to her; she is willing both to cheat at cards and to "grant the Favour" to a generous man. She tells her lover, Garnish, that, "as my Lord says, there's no true Friend, but Mony—." Garnish protests and she adds, "And your self. But let us get as much Mony as we can; 'twill secure your Friendship to me" (22). Her distrust of Garnish's loyalty reflects her cynicism and her own untrustworthiness—she is willing to cheat him for money as quickly as anybody else.

The extent of Lady Trickitt's self-serving independence is defined by her relationships with men in the play. Her attentions to Granger are solely in hopes of remuneration; when he presumes to offer an assignation, she arranges for him to meet another woman, Lady Susan. His embarrassment and discomfort are punishment for his stinginess; after all, Lady Trickitt muses, "How could he imagine I would allow him a Favour, when he had giv'n me such a reason to believe he did not think it worth paying for?" (71). Lady Trickitt is something more than an errant wife—she is a woman who values her freedom of action so highly that she cannot be the sexual plaything of gallants, as earlier wanton wives were, nor allow of any relationships which encroach upon that freedom. When Garnish is jealous and suspicious of her relationship with Granger, she reminds him that "matters between you and me are entirely depending upon our good Liking and Pleasure" and that "the most desparate Jealousie of this kind lies within the remedy of Parting." In one of the play's most telling speeches, she provides Garnish, and us, with a manifesto of female free gallantry:

Sir, I won't be suspected, I won't be enquir'd into: A husband can do no more; and I have enough of one Husband and his ill Humours at home, I thank you, ever to allow of a Husband abroad to torment me. Perhaps you think I can't break with you; I wou'd have you to know, Sir, I can, and will break with you and Fifty more, rather than break one Hour's Rest for any of you. I'll change as often as I shift my Cloaths, but I'll light upon a Man that has Sense enough to value his own Pleasure, without invading mine. If I depended upon you indeed, and there were no body else to be had, you might tie me to your own Terms, but, make us thankful, there's roving room enough in this dear Town: I can provide my self, I warrant you.
     A Mistress is a name implies Command:
     Nor shall the Scepter fail within my Hand:
     But if you wou'd take back the Pow'r you gave,
     Marry the Woman you wou'd make a Slave.
                                        (73)

Like a jealous husband, Garnish, cured when he sees her reject Granger later in the play, petitions for reinstatement; but, when she takes him back, it is clearly on her own terms. She views marriage principally as a restraint upon women, and she is able to maintain the freedom of a man by avoiding her actual marriage as much as possible and the conditions of marriage in her extramarital affairs fully. In effect, this is to make Garnish wife to her husband, if he wishes to continue the relationship.

     The wife in the Malepert marriage sees the world much as Lady Trickitt does, not by inclination but by training. Under the guidance of Mrs. Wishwell, who was given charge of her breeding, she was married to Lord Malepert because his wealth and folly made him an ideal cuckold. Since then, Mrs. Wishwell has engineered a profitable affair between Lady Malepert and Lord Lofty, another character who never appears but whose off-stage presence provokes comment and action on stage. In the course of the play Mrs. Wishwell attempts to substitute Sir Ruff Rancounter, a boorish but wealthy country knight, for Lord Lofty, whose powers at court have faded, making him less generous a lover and less helpful to the advancement of Lord Malepert. Deliberately, Mrs. Wishwell has created liaisons for Lady Malepert which pose no threat of serious involvement—Lord Lofty is old; Sir Ruff is crude; Lord Malepert is a giddy fool—and she continually attempts to keep her from Gayman, a gallant suitor for whom Lady Malepert once had great feeling.

Unlike Lady Trickitt, Lady Malepert is capable of love but her nature is eroded by her experiences in the world. Southerne reveals her character in a soliloquy after she has had sexual intercourse with Gayman, whom she thought was her new keeper, Sir Ruff:

I have slept away my Life, my better Part of it, my Life of Love: He's gone from me: Was this an Hour of Rest? Sleep had been welcome in a Husband's bed; but in a Lover's Arms! . . . he stole away, in everything showing his Care of me: How cou'd Sir *Ruff* do this? O Love! what canst thou not do in a Woman's Heart! that brutal thing, whom, as I thought, I loath'd, thy gentle Fires hath softned by degrees, and melted into *Gayman*: Night be still my Friend, let me not see him, and I will think it was my *Gayman* still. (75)[4]

Lady Malepert shares with Lady Trickitt the negative expectations about a husband's role but is unlike her in the highly emotional response she brings to the experience. However, Lady Malepert's ecstasy is solely based on Gayman's performance in bed; sexual satisfaction is the only alternative she has to mercenary indifference. But Gayman's belief that she would have been as ardent with Sir Ruff makes him reject her, and consequently she loses any opportunity she might have had for an emotionally reciprocal relationship. She remains, in the final act, under the charge of Mrs. Wishwell.

In some ways, Mrs. Wishwell is the central element of the milieu of this play. She is similar to Mrs. Witwoud in *The Wives Excuse* in her maliciousness and deceit, but her motives are more powerfully expressed. She resents her age, her loss of beauty, the hypocrisy of those who flatter her to court Lady Malepert, but she wants that flattery and takes spiteful delight in the power she wields. She first appears in Act II at her toilet, rejecting her maid Christian's suggestion of a wash:

I use the Wash! a Woman turn'd of fifty was ne'er design'd to be lookt upon: I may Wash and Patch, and please my self; cheat my Hopes with the
daily expence of Plaister and Repairs; no Body will take the Tenement off
my Hands. Men use us, as we use our Spectacles, to draw the Object nearer
to the Sense: Indeed we are the fittest Means to guide and light their dark
Designs home to their Ends on younger Women. No matter for the
Character; I live by them, and they shall Love by me. While I am Mistress
of Malepert's Beauty, I am not very sensible of the loss of my own: For her
sake I will be courted: I have so many howd'ye's, and Invitations in the
Morning upon her Account; so many Visits in the Afternoon; and so many
Bows in the Drawing-Room at Night.   (23)

Recognizing the danger to herself in Gayman, whom Lady
Malepert likes, she solicits Sir Ruff instead. "While I can keep her
to Men, where she can like nothing but their Mony, I'm safe.
Therefore that Brute shall have her." She later describes Sir Ruff to
the lady as "a Beast, to bear the Burthen of your Expences upon your
Pleasure" (30) and compares him to her husband: "They're Beasts
alike," reinforcing a central idea of the play—the mercenary base of
both marriages and intrigues. She advises Lady Malepert to ignore
her inclinations: "If you allow them to get the better of you, you are
undone: There are a great many pretty Gentlemen to be had: but
what will you get by any of 'em in the End? Just so much Experience,
and Repentance for your Pains. . . . No, no, no Love: We'll learn
that of the Men—For Love is Nature's Appetite diseas'd: where we
have no Concern, we're always pleas'd" (30). Here Mrs. Wishwell
completely reverses and distorts the traditional view of love, but her
philosophy of loveless relationships is not far from being a description
of the socially acceptable marriage of convenience. The rejection of
Lady Malepert by Gayman provides Mrs. Wishwell's ultimate
triumph.

III   *The Rewards of Intrigue and the Play's Men*

For the men of the play sexual intrigue is no more rewarding than
for the women. Sir Ruff is as cold-blooded as Mrs. Wishwell about
the affair with Lady Malepert he is spending so much to initiate:
"Not that I think her any better than her Chambermaid: 'Tis the
Woman does my Business, and not the Lady: I had rather have a
prudent Practiser of the Trade, to use as I think fit; than a
Gentlewoman (that only does it now and then, for her diversion) to

use me as she pleases. But, you know, a Man in this Town is no
Body, without the Reputation of a Quality-Intrigue: And all that I
do it for, is to talk of it in Company" (31). His motives are those of
Wilding in *The Wives Excuse*, more crudely expressed.

Sir Symphony, too, seems to have expended much time and
money to bring about affairs. He tells Gayman of his "Catalogue of
the Ladies I visit, Ogle, and say soft things to: Seven and fifty,
Widows, Wives, and Maids: And if I don't succeed with some of
'em; I have been a civil Person to little purpose"(42). In Act V he
expresses a weariness with masquerades:

'Tis losing one's Labour always upon other men's Mistresses; when you
have waited upon a Gentlewoman thro' the Ceremonies of the Night, and
think of going home with her, tho' you have cram'd her Pockets as full of
Sweetmeats as they can hold, her own Spark appears in the Morning; beats
you, perhaps, for offering to lead her to her Coach, and forces you to walk
home, Ankle deep, in your *Turkish* habit.

(79)

The description carries the weight of experience; Sir Symphony has
been playing out of his league.

But the dissatisfaction with the way of the world is expressed with
particular force by the more conventional rake figures, Granger and
Gayman. Granger is a plain dealer, fully aware that his interest in
Lady Trickitt is sexual and that he expects to use her like the trollop
he thinks she is. He learns instead that he cannot use her without
paying a far larger price than he is willing to pay. Granger is similar
to Wycherley's Manly in his hatred of hypocrisy and his desire to in-
flict a sexual punishment upon a deceitful woman; but Lady
Trickitt outsmarts him, and he has no Fidelia to fall back on, as
Manly had. He has learned a lesson about himself, however, and
about his own ability to be corrupted by this world he despises. As
when earlier he turns to befriending Lord Lofty after he falls from
power and is rejected by the beau monde, so Granger stands alone
at the end of the play, observing of this world that " 'Tis as much as
a Man can do, to secure a Reputation, in his own keeping; he need
not venture it in a Woman's."

Gayman, too, suffers a reversal. He thinks it would be enough to
possess Lady Malepert, to win her by his charm rather than by
money, but after outwitting Sir Ruff and possessing her in his place,
he cannot bring himself to ignore what the fact of her willingness
implies. He muses:

Now can't I help thinking of Sir *Ruff*, and destroying the Memory of this
Night's Pleasures, by calling to mind that they were all design'd for
another. Can't I be contented with the Enjoyment of a delicious woman,
without reflecting, that any body else might have had her as well as I? 'Tis
an impertinent Curiosity in our Natures, that when we have discover'd as
much as we can, to please us, will always drive us upon something to find
Fault with: Curiosity did I call it? Nay, gad, there's Ingratitude in the bot-
tom on't, I believe: for 'tis the way of the World, in other Favors too, to
lessen those Obligations, as much as we can, which we han't in our Honesty
to return. Pox, I hate to be ungrateful: But I can't be ungrateful here, if I
wou'd; for there was nothing design'd for me of the Benefits I receiv'd:

(74)

In the course of that speech Gayman comes to the realization of the
emptiness of his relationship with Lady Malepert; achieving her
bed has not brought him triumph because for her consummation
has no significance. The moment he realizes that this liaison is
devoid of feeling, he begins to turn toward accepting the "high way
of matrimony" with Maria. She warns him— "you may repent your
rashness"—but his reply reveals his awareness of the differences in
the relationships with Lady Malepert and Maria: "I may repent of
some things that are past: But I can never do any thing with you, to
repent of" (85).
    For all parties involved, the ethic of free-gallantry is unsatisfying,
bringing no pleasure, merely financial or social gain, at the price of
subjugation or disillusionment. Those who triumph, Lady Trickitt
and Mrs. Wishwell, do so because they invest nothing of themselves
in the matter; only the rakes, who in earlier comedies are smug
predators, realize the folly of free-gallantry. Gayman chooses an
alternative to Garnish's dependence and Granger's isolation, but the
alternative is not without qualifications. Even as Gayman and Maria
accept one another, Sir Symphony and Lady Susan, two conspicuous failures on this social-sexual merry-go-round, do likewise.
Lady Susan's pursuit of Granger had made her continually rebuff
Sir Symphony, but when Granger flatly rejects her, she finally turns
to Sir Symphony, the old maid's last prayer; for both of them it is
better to take any rather than fail altogether. And in the midst of
these marriage preparations two minor characters, Siam and her
husband, Captain Drydrubb, enter. The inadequacy of their
marriage is suggested both by his name and by his complaint that
her grievance is that "you would have me begin to propagate, like a
Patriarch, at threescore and try to do good in my Generation" (86).

He claims both are past it, and his insane jealousy and general boorishness finally force her to offer him a separate maintenance, his hope since their marriage: "I marry'd you only to maintain me" (86).

With the panoply of marriage which he presents to us, Southerne must surely not expect us to be wholly satisfied with Gayman's motives for marriage. Still, by comparison with the indifference of the Trickitts, the self-destructiveness of the Maleperts, and the incompatibility of the Drydrubbs, the essential compatibility of both couples, Gayman and Maria, and Sir Symphony and Lady Susan, seems to hold out the hope that happy marriages can still occur.

IV   *Critical Responses*

Like *The Wives Excuse, The Maid's Last Prayer* is a scathing social document as well as a powerful, highly structured play; more biting and tough-minded than the earlier play, it advances Southerne's ability to delineate the psychology or pathology of his characters. The passages quoted above demonstrate how fully the playwright has seen the complexity of these situations and the complexity of response they require. In effective epiphanies throughout the play, most of the characters reveal motives demanding of sympathy, sometimes in the middle of distaste. Yet Southerne's depiction of a sordid milieu has too often been seen as his advocacy of it, a crass attempt to outdo libertine writers in smuttiness. Dodds, the most unsympathetic of Southerne scholars, excoriated the play, stating that here Southerne "sinks to a level of dullness below even that of *The Wives Excuse.*"[5] Nicoll also talks of his sinking below his earlier play, but has some good words for individual scenes. Some of them, he feels, "are worthy of Congreve himself, but they are buried in a mass of uninteresting padding which the author seemed unable to refine."[6] Motteux, on the other hand, commended it in the *Gentleman's Journal,* saying: "It discovers much Knowledge of the Town in its Author; and its Wit and purity of Diction are particularly commended."[7] Contemporary critics have valued the play more highly, and Hume's assessment seems more on target: "The play is splendidly brisk, an icy account of corruption, and a beautiful example of hard comedy at its best."[8]

Critics of Restoration drama early in this century tended to judge comedy by nineteenth-century standards—they viewed the conventions uniformly and too often could not recognize the variations of execution used by diverse playwrights. Southerne's contemporaries could see more clearly what he was about, and it is more likely that they objected less to his attack on free-gallantry than they did his refusal to allow them to enjoy it vicariously in his plays. Yet Southerne's concern with the psychology of his characters, evidenced as early as his first two plays, suggests that as much as he could not write plays condoning free-gallantry, neither could he write simplistic reforming comedies.[9]

In the discussion of his comedies here and in Chapter 4, it is evident that the problematics of marriage interested Southerne from his earliest plays and that in *The Wives Excuse* in particular and in *The Maid's Last Prayer* as well his powers of dramatic construction and characterization could at last provide the appropriate vehicle to carry the intensity he brought to his theme. As has been suggested already, the importance of these two comedies, apart from their value as powerful specimens of dramatic art, lies in the way they trigger a chain reaction of comedies incisively analyzing marriage; in a sense, *The Provok'd Wife* of Vanbrugh is an incremental reevaluation of the central triangle of *The Wives Excuse*, and *The Beaux' Stratagem* of Farquhar a somewhat more extended and overt reevaluation because of how it adds to and alters Vanbrugh's triangle. But for Southerne in 1693, the comedy of marriage offered unpromising prospects, since his best efforts had been unable to find an audience. His response to the experience is suggested by the Latin motto on the title page of *The Maid's Last Prayer*: *"Valeat res ludicra, si me Palma negata, macrum; donata reducit opimum"* (Farewell the comic stage, if denial of the palm sends me home lean, its bestowal plump).[10] Leaving the comic mode, he turned back to serious drama, where, nevertheless, he did not abandon the themes which had occupied him so much in comedy.

CHAPTER 6

The Fatal Marriage

I *Theatrical History*

*T*HE *Fatal Marriage, or, The Innocent Adultery* is the first of Southerne's plays to have an extensive theatrical history, one studded with successful moments. It had its premiere in February 1694, with Elizabeth Barry in the role of Isabella; John Downes credited that role, as well as those of Otway's Monimia and Belvidera, as having "gain'd her the Name of Famous Mrs. *Barry,* both at Court and City; for when ever She Acted any of those three parts, she forc'd Tears from the Eyes of her Auditory, especially those who have any Sense of Pity for the Distress't."[1] The reception of the play was immediately enthusiastic and secured Southerne's reputation among his contemporaries; Motteaux wrote in the *Gentleman's Journal:* "Mr. Southern's new Play call'd *The Fatal Marriage, or, The Innocent Adultery,* has been so kindly receiv'd, that you are by this time no stranger to its merit. As the world has done it justice, and it is above my praise, I need not expatiate upon that subject."[2] An unidentified writer of March 1694, while reveling in the concurrent discouragement of Congreve's *The Double Dealer* and outright rejection of Dryden's *Love Triumphant,* had high praise for the play, providing us at the same time with evidence of the financial success for which Southerne came to be well known. He says the play is "not only the best that author ever writt, but is generally admired for one of the greatest ornaments of the stage, and the most entertaining play has appeared upon it these 7 years. . . . I never saw Mrs. Barry act with so much passion as she does in it. I could not forbear being moved even to tears to see her act. Never was poet better rewarded or incouraged by the town; for besides an extraordinary full house, which brought him about 140£, 50 noblemen, among whom My Lord Winchelsea was one, gave him guineas apiece, and the printer 36£ for his copy."[3]

From that rousing beginning, the play maintained its popularity for the next century and a half, both as a vehicle for leading ladies and a certain box-office success. As the tastes of the times changed, other hands were always ready to make it conform. David Garrick, advised by Francis Gentleman, removed the comic plot of the play and premiered a shortened version with himself as Biron and Susannah Maria Cibber as Isabella December 2, 1757. In the same month he published *Isabella, or, The Fatal Marriage;* it was known by that title throughout the remainder of its stage history.[4] Toward the end of the eighteenth century John Philip Kemble as Biron, Charles Kemble as Carlos, and Sarah Kemble Siddons as Isabella were successful in Kemble's adaptation of Garrick's version.[5] In addition to London success, Fanny Kemble triumphed as Isabella on the Edinburgh stage in 1830, before an audience which included Sir Walter Scott.[6] The play was performed frequently in the United States between 1783 and 1843, with performances in New York, Boston, Philadelphia, New Orleans, Hartford, Baltimore, and Washington recorded.[7] Typically the leading actresses of the period chose the play for performances on the days of their benefits. Although it was no longer played after the first half of the nineteenth century, it was anthologized in England as late as 1883.

II *Southerne and Behn*

Southerne drew upon Aphra Behn's novel *The History of the Nun, or, The Fair Vow-Breaker* as a source for the main plot of the play; but, as he himself says in the dedication, the borrowings are little more than hints. Behn's novel details at length the childhood of Isabella in a convent, her education in worldly behavior, her choice of holy vows, and her eventual elopement from the nunnery to marry Henault. Henault's father disowns him, until he agrees to go fight the Turks, where he vanishes at the battle of Candia. She again meets Villenoys, a former suitor, marries him, and lives happily until Henault returns. For a series of complicated reasons, centering on a fear of returning to poverty with Henault, the shame of having two husbands, the guilt over not mourning Henault longer, worry about losing Villenoys, and her lost love for Henault, Isabella smothers him and tricks Villenoys into disposing of the body. But her fear of discovery is so great that she sews the sack containing the body to Villenoy's coat, so that when he throws it into the river, he himself is pulled in and drowned. Eventually she is found out and executed. Thus the story deals with the pathology of a murderess and serves as a warning to vow-breakers.

Southerne's version is far more concerned with the psychology of a woman who has suffered continually and who commits adultery and bigamy innocently. His play begins with Biron (Henault of the novel) nearly seven years missing, Villeroy still Isabella's persistent and devoted suitor, and Isabella herself impoverished and continually besieged by her creditors. Biron's father, Count Baldwin, has never forgiven her for abandoning her nun's vows and marrying his son; indeed, Baldwin is so hard-hearted that he agrees to provide for his grandson only if Isabella will promise never to see him again. Thus her financial circumstances as well as her respect and affection for Villeroy incline her toward marriage; and she is further pushed in that direction by Carlos, Biron's brother, the only one who knows that Biron is still alive. He has been intercepting letters from Biron, at present a Turkish slave, and conniving to become his father's sole heir. Eventually Isabella and Villeroy are married and Biron returns, just when Villeroy has left to visit a dying friend. Isabella is driven to distraction by her dilemma, almost to the point of killing the sleeping Biron, who is still unaware she has remarried. Shortly after, Biron is ambushed by Carlos and his henchmen and fatally wounded, although Villeroy rescues him. Biron dies and Isabella stabs herself. Carlos is brought to justice and Baldwin shown the hard-heartedness of his behavior.

This is quite a different story from Behn's, which is why Southerne's claim to having taken only a hint is just. Southerne's Isabella is a suffering heroine driven relentlessly and unjustly to her death by circumstances beyond her control. Although Link says of Behn's tale, "The moral the story presents is spurious and imposed—a mere excuse for a romantic and improbable tale," it does continually suggest that there is a fate which punishes vow-breakers.[8] But only Baldwin feels that way in Southerne's play, and he is proved to be wrong through the action. In fact, her death is more directly attributable to the hard-heartedness of Baldwin and the cold-bloodedness of Carlos than to her own actions.

Thus, while Southerne's plot may be nominally drawn from Behn's novel, its spirit is rather remote from it—resembling more the great tragedies of Thomas Otway, particularly *The Orphan*, where Monimia is continually surrounded by a degenerate environment which ultimately destroys her. Southerne's play is not so sordid or oppressive as Otway's; but, as in *The Orphan*, the fate which overtakes the heroine is largely in the hands of the men of the play's milieu. Not coincidentally, although the plays were produced fifteen years apart, both drew on the talents of Elizabeth Barry and were in effect written for her.

The Fatal Marriage is pathetic tragedy in exactly the terms that Otway and Banks presented it, except that it is far more domestic in setting. There is little foreign color here, though the play is set in Brussels, and little to suggest affairs of greater moment than the personal affairs of the participants. The action centers on marriage, adultery, inheritance, and familial relationships, with affairs of state distant and remote; indeed, all the problems of the play are traceable to the inflexibility of parents.

III   *Isabella and the Forces against Her*

The plight of Isabella depends upon the behavior of Count Baldwin. Although the church has forgiven her, Baldwin has not. His insistence that his son redeem himself in his father's eyes by military service results in Biron's disappearance and years of slavery following the siege of Candia. But Baldwin holds Isabella responsible and continually opposes her. Southerne opens Isabella's story by showing her as a wife who would be loyal to a husband she cannot bring herself to believe is dead, who would provide for her son and herself, but who cannot escape the consequences of poverty. Pursued by creditors, importuned by Villeroy, she turns to Baldwin for help, enduring the arrogance of his porter, Samson, before the compassion of the Nurse gains her admittance. Baldwin, however, is moved to help her child primarily to punish her by depriving her of him and casts out his porter and nurse for admitting her, thus adding them to her burdens. It is this increased responsibility and the expectation of no other relief that finally convinces her to marry Villeroy.

Like Mrs. Friendall under similarly beleaguered circumstances, Isabella operates here—as elsewhere—out of complex motives. Torn by loyalty to her husband, respect for Villeroy, and her sense of tribulation, she tries to avoid the appearance of coming to Villeroy out of need rather than love. She is, like Mrs. Friendall, aware of her own sense of honor; and when she finally accepts him, encouraged by her dependents, her brother-in-law, Carlos, and

Villeroy himself, the speech in which she moves toward acceptance
is fraught with hesitations and qualifications:

> My Pleasures are
> Bury'd, and cold in my dead Husband's Grave.
> And I should wrong the Truth, my self, and you,
> To say that I can ever love again.
> I owe this Declaration to my self:
> But as a Proof that I owe all to you,
> If after what I've said, you can resolve
> To think me worth your Love—Where am I going?
>
> . . .
>
> You should not ask me now, nor should I grant.
> I am so much oblig'd, that to consent
> Wou'd want a Name to recommend the Gift.
> 'Twould shew me poor, indebted, and compell'd,
> Designing, mercenary; and I know
> You would not wish to think I could be bought.
>
> (V. II, p. 123)

Isabella's distress over her predicament, expressed in a suspicion of
her own motives, displays the complexity of her nature. At the same
time that it demonstrates her unselfishness, her speech foreshadows
her greater distress when her forbodings about a second marriage,
so lightly dismissed by the others, all prove true.

Biron's return sets off a chain reaction of self-incrimination,
despair, and guilt within Isabella. In one of the strong set speeches
which made this part so popular with actresses, Southerne explores
her tortured state of mind:

> I'll but say my Prayers, and follow you—
> My Prayers! no, I must ne'er Pray again.
> Prayers have their Blessings to reward our Hopes:
> But I have nothing left to hope for more.
> What Heav'n could give, I have enjoy'd; but now
> The baneful Planet rises on my Fate,
> And what's to come, is a long Line of Woe;
> Yet I may shorten it—
> I promis'd him to follow—him!
> Is he without a Name? *Biron*, my Husband:
> To follow him to Bed—my Husband! ha!

What then is *Villeroy?* But yesterday
That very Bed receiv'd him for its Lord;
Yet a warm Witness to my broken Vows,
To send another to usurp his room.
O Biron! hadst thou come but one day sooner,
I wou'd have follow'd thee through Beggary,
Through all the Chances of this weary Life,
Wander'd the many ways of wretchedness
With thee, to find a hospitable Grave;
For that's the only Bed that's left me now. (Weeping)
—What's to be done—for something must be done.
Two Husbands! yet not one! by both enjoy'd,
And yet a Wife to neither! hold my Brain—
This is to live in common! Very Beasts,
That welcome all they meet, make just such Wives.
                                                  (155)

The speech builds from static self-pity through a series of
epiphanies—such as that about her refusal to name her
husband—into a frenzy of self-accusation and finally imagined
public infamy, fearing "the dividing Tongues of *Biron's* Wrongs,
and *Villeroy's* Resentments" will tear asunder reputation and also
dreading "old *Baldwin's* Triumph in my Ruin." With this welter of
ills weighing her down, she begins to contemplate suicide.

The soliloquy quoted here is a pivotal speech, marking the
turning point for Isabella's temperament, the moment she begins a
descent leading her inevitably to death. Southerne handles the
scene naturally and carefully, endowing her speech with the
awareness of complex motives which is typical of his best
characterization. We see here the reasons why there is no easy
retreat for Isabella. Although Samson the porter claims at one point
that there is no problem, that under the law "the Man must have
his Mare again," it is not the legalities of the situation that are at
issue. Southerne is exploring how much suffering the mind can endure and even Biron acknowledges to the nurse that Isabella has
cause for her "brain to turn." Although at one moment she considers murdering Biron and continually contemplates suicide, ultimately it is the death of Biron on top of everything else that finally
provokes her to kill herself.

In another world, we are led to believe, Isabella might have lived
happily with either Biron or Villeroy. Both are exemplary male

figures, righteous men and steadfast lovers. They are much alike, both devoted to Isabella, optimistic, almost impervious to dread; they enhance Isabella's role and share with her the crushing blows of fate: both come to talk of suicide and at the play's end Biron is dead and Villeroy broken.

But the world of this play is dominated by two others, Biron's father, Count Baldwin, and his younger brother, Carlos. Baldwin is a vindictive old man, relentlessly unpitying, who deprives his oldest son of his inheritance because he married without his consent, and who unconsciously fosters the hopes of the younger son to such a degree that he will stoop to any crime to realize them. Carlos is part of a long line of younger sons in Restoration drama; indeed, a good many of the protagonists of Restoration comedy are younger sons who need to marry well because they are penniless. In Carlos the art mirroring Restoration life reflects the effect of the callousness underlying the law of inheritance. Ultimately, Isabella is the victim of both father and son, Baldwin continually driving her deeper into debt and despair, Carlos concealing from her Biron's being alive and forcing her into the marriage which will disinherit her son and Biron's. Moreoever, it is Carlos's final act of desperation, the murder of Biron, which initiates the final catastrophe, Isabella's death.

That we are to view Isabella as blameless throughout is made clear by the closing words of the play, when Count Baldwin turns to his orphaned grandson, declaring, "My flinty Heart, That Barren Rock on which thy Father starv'd, Opens its Springs of Nourishment for thee." His acknowledgment of his own fault absolves Isabella for the guilt that might be attached to her actions:

> O had I pardon'd my poor Biron's Fault!
> His first, his only Fault, this had not been.
> To erring Youth there's some Compassion due;
> But while with Rigour you their Crimes pursue,
> What's their Misfortune, is a Crime in you.
> Hence learn offending Children to forgive:
> Leave Punishment to Heav'n, 'tis Heav'n's Prerogative.
> (174)

As with his earlier heroines, so with Isabella, Southerne clearly sees the woman as a victim in her society, not a guilty party.[9]

IV   *Parallels in the Comic Action*

The tragic action of the play is fairly simple and straightforward and sufficiently independent that the comic action of the play barely intrudes upon it. Nonetheless the comic subplot of the play is designed to support the tragic main plot. The extent to which the design is Southerne's is clear if we compare it to his possible source material, John Fletcher's play *The Night Walker, or, The Little Thief,* itself loosely derived from Boccaccio's *The Decameron,* Third Day, Eighth Tale. Boccaccio tells a bawdy fabliau in which a rakish abbot makes a man believe himself dead and in Purgatory while the abbot enjoys his wife. The husband is released and "restored to life" only after his wife is pregnant and his jealousy is cured, thus ensuring a successful continuing relationship with the abbot. Fletcher's version is really quite different: when Algripe the usurer is confronted with the fear of death and hell, an angel gives him a chance to surrender the ingénue to her true love and make restitution for the wickedness of his life; the angel is really Algripe's lost love, Alath, in disguise, and the ending is happy.[10]

Southerne may have known these materials but if so he used only the central premises and modified his narrative material to parallel the serious plot of his play. In his version Fernando is equivalent to Baldwin, a jealous and possessive husband, a stern and suspicious father. Fabian, his son, hopes to make him more generous by convincing him that he has taken holy orders; like Carlos, he also hopes to eliminate rivals for his father's money by helping his sister, Victoria, elope with Frederick. He also seems moved to help his stepmother, Julia, gain her freedom through an affair with Carlos. But the women in the action have their own plans. When Victoria escapes with Frederick, disguised as a man, she will become neither his mistress nor his wife until she wins her father's approval—she is too conscious of the hardships which can ensue following the final disobedience. And Julia, while she is flattered by Carlos's advances, has no intention of granting him her favors; she remains a loyal wife certain life will be better when her husband is cured. The cure involves drugging Fernando, beating him like a soul in purgatory, and then bringing him back from the dead with a new appreciation of his family and of life itself. He finds his wife faithful to his memory and abandons jealousy; he finds his daughter still virginal and unmarried and grants her and Frederick his blessing; he has been admonished for his penuriousness with his son and promises him half his estate immediately. At the end he moralizes, "Husbands who doubt my story, / May find in Jealousie their Purgatory."

In both plots stern fathers oppose love matches: Baldwin's opposition forces Biron to war and precipitates the catastrophe of the tragedy; Fernando's forces Victoria to elope. In both plots younger brothers connive for money. In both the father figures reform, Fernando in time to prevent disaster in his family, Baldwin too late for Biron and Isabella but in time to save their child. The main plot is a tragedy of errors magnified by greed and vindictiveness; the subplot is a comedy of greed and suspicion where cunning and prudence produce a happy ending. The comic plot ends in Act IV, however, and Frederick, as friend to Carlos, appears in a serious role in the rest of the play, which follows the tragic action from the return of Biron to the conclusion. Thus the comic parallels do little to moderate the intensity of the tragic action, and possibly, in the last emotional rush, seem superfluous to the design of the play.

Multiple plots, of course, were not unusual in tragedy, occurring frequently in Elizabethan plays and rather successfully in one of Dryden's best plays, *Don Sebastian* (1689). Southerne certainly has precedent for his multiple plotting; and indeed the construction of the play is not unlike that of *The Disappointment*, although there the parallel plots are more tightly interrelated. In *The Fatal Marriage* the comic plot is lively and amusing, offering some deftly handled farcical scenes, like the planting of a letter to Victoria on her father by the wily servant, Jaquelin, or the disastrous attempt at elopement, a hectic and frantic slapstick scene. Nonetheless, the comic plot was an early and frequent objection to the play.

V *The Critical Response*

Garrick summarized the flow of contemporary opinion in his edition of 1758. In the advertisement he writes: "The Tragic Part of this Play has been always esteemed extremely Natural and Interesting; and it would probably, like some others, have produc'd its full Effect, notwithstanding the Intervention of the Comic Scenes that are mixed with it: The Editor therefore, would not have thought of removing them, if they had not been exceptionable in themselves, not only as indelicate, but as immoral."[11] There seems to have been widespread agreement over the indelicacy of the comic plot: *The Companion to the Playhouse* complained of it and

noted, in a metaphor common to this play, that "some one,
however, has since purified the Ore from its Dross, by clearing the
Play of all the comic Part, excepting so much of the Characters of
the Nurse and Porter, as are inseparable from the Affairs of
Isabella."[12] It was in this version that audiences saw the great
triumphs of actresses for the next century.

However, by 1817, when he published an introduction to it in his
multi-volume anthology of British drama, Richard Cumberland had
taken a far darker view of the play. He complained that, as an in-
tervening character, that of Carlos "has more demands upon it than
nature and probability can well provide for" and that Baldwin
seemed too cruel. "Southerne has mingled so much dross with gold,
that it has been necessary to refine it over and over again, before it
could be made a decent vehicle to exhibit the fine acting which,
from the time of Mrs. Cibber to the present, has been the sole support of this melo-dramatic tragi-comedy." The worst point in the
play for Cumberland is the conclusion, where Southerne "appears
like a bedlamite broken loose from his chains"; he "commits
murders without meaning, and instead of making madness horrible,
he makes horror mad." Worst of all, he "lets his heroine, in whose
sorrows we had sympathized, take leave of life, and preface the
dreadful act of self-murder by the most impious disavowal of
Heaven's justice, uttering these horrid blasphemies when she
plunges the dagger into her heart. . . . What could be in
Southerne's mind when he conceiv'd this passage, puzzles me to
conjecture. It would have been outrageous blasphemy even in a dying Pagan, and insanity itself cannot apologize for it." His sum-
mation: "That there are passages of exquisite and pathetic simplici-
ty in this motley drama, no reader can fail to acknowledge; but
every critic will be unanimous in condemning it as a most faulty
and imperfect composition."[13]

Cumberland's objections are the most extreme ever written about
the play, but they suggest how even a play widely admired for its
ability to provoke empathy in its audience—even one already revised to meet changing tastes—could not hope to be always in
vogue. Within a dozen years of Cumberland's tirade, the play left
the British stage, although it flourished for a while longer in
America. At roughly the same time, however, Genest claimed that
"the tragic plot of this play is probable, the distress domestic, and
the language in general pathetic—the comic plot is very fair," thus
disagreeing with Cumberland.[14] And if it appeared no more on the

stage, it was nonetheless a staple in anthologies of British drama.[15]

The long history of the play on stage and in print testifies to its power with viewing and reading audiences. Dodds offers a sound explanation: "He had to a greater degree than most a power over the affections of the human heart. With a simple directness remarkably free from bombast he could wring the last degree of pathos from such a spectacle of unmerited suffering as Isabella's. Here is found at once his true worth and the secret of his popularity for nearly a century and a half."[16] For Dodds, Southerne's contribution to the development of domestic tragedy, particularly in the focus on the suffering heroine, is his chief merit as a dramatist. To a degree, of course, he is right: as others point out, Southerne is the bridge between Otway and Rowe, between the pathetic tragedy of the Restoration and the sentimental tragedy of the eighteenth century. Nicoll writes: "In a strange and artistic manner here Southerne has united the spirit of the tragedy of blood with the spirit of the new sentimental and pathetic drama, still with a few reminiscences of the heroic stage. Sentiment rather than horror, however, looms over the fatal bride, tossed on a tormented sea of diabolically-human intrigue."[17]

More recently, the play has come to be appreciated in its original form, for its own merits rather than for its role in literary history. Scouten writes, "Southerne does employ a comic subplot to great advantage. Instead of trying to sustain the same high level of emotional intensity, as Lee tried to do, Southerne inserts his comic scenes functionally, and by relief and contrast is able to heighten his sad story."[18] Hume supports this view of the play: "Southerne's play is as fine as pathetic drama gets. Not only is its construction beautifully done, but the comic variety is both welcome and thematically pointed."[19] Both these views acknowledge the sense of artistic purpose in the double plot which earlier critics did not see.

What Hume calls Southerne's "penchant for psychological observation and study of motivation" is the organizing principle behind the play. As in the comedies these are presented vividly, in striking scenes. Yet they seem, as they did in his earlier serious dramas, still part of the artifice behind the play. In Hume's terms, "Southerne has become an extremely polished playwright. *The Fatal Marriage* has everything a play needs to be great—except internal *raison d'être* for the tragedy. The pain we feel is that elicited by a gruesomely enacted accident—and so we may be left tearful, but we are never deeply moved."[20] But these are very much the terms

of Restoration comedy itself—the emphasis on the individual moment, the focus on the pathetic—and in achieving command of
them, Southerne solidly established himself among the chief tragic
writers of his age.

CHAPTER 7

Oroonoko

I   Oroonoko's *Long Life upon the Stage*

OROONOKO was first performed sometime in November 1695 and probably published on December 16, 1695. At the time of its premiere the United Company had dissolved and Betterton had led Elizabeth Barry, Anne Bracegirdle, and the veterans of the company to a different theater, depriving Southerne of a number of the finest actors he had relied upon in the past. Nonetheless the original cast was a smashing success. John Verbruggen took the role of Oroonoko, and it made his reputation; Cibber claimed that "the late Marquess of *Hallifax* order'd *Oroonoko* to be taken from *George Powel*, saying to Mr. *Southern*, the Author,—That *Jack* was the unpolish'd Hero, and wou'd do it best."[1] Powell took the role of Aboan. The female lead, Imoinda, was played by Jane Rogers, and the Widow Lackit by Frances Knight; Charlotte Welldon, the woman disguised as a man, was created by Susannah Mountfort Verbruggen, who had originated the role of Sir Anthony Love. This cast brought the play immediate acclaim and *Oroonoko* was to be a staple of the repertory for nearly 150 years. The *London Stage* records 315 performances between its premiere and the close of the eighteenth century, and its longevity continued into the first third of the nineteenth.

Like *the Fatal Marriage*, *Oroonoko*'s long life did not escape emendation. Toward the middle of the eighteenth century the comic plot of the play was adapted as a droll. Together with parts of Fletcher's *Monsieur Thomas*, it was shortened into two acts as *The Sexes Mismatch'd, or, a New Way to Get a Husband*, and printed among several others in *The Strollers Pacquet Open'd* (1742). Later the comic plot was jettisoned by others who had always objected to its presence, among them John Hawkesworth, who published a version in 1759, and Francis Gentleman, who produced his in 1760. David Garrick, who had first appeared on the stage as Aboan, under

the name Lydall, used Hawkesworth's transformation.[2] It was in
this amended version that the play continued to be popular for the
rest of the century. With Margaret Somerville as Imoinda, Edmund
Kean played Oroonoko to the applause of William Hazlitt January
26, 1817.[3] The play was also produced in Edinburgh and Dublin,
and often performed in America between 1792 and Junius Brutus
Booth's revival in New York in 1832. From that performance, the
play languished until August 3, 1932, when Ralph Richardson took
the title role at the Malvern Festival.[4]

The printing history of the play is equally remarkable. Dodds
noted fifty-seven printings of the play by 1933, counting
Hawkesworth's amended version as a variation of Southerne's text.[5]
There was also a corruption of the play by John Ferriar as *The
Prince of Angola* in 1788, more fully to fit the tastes of the
abolitionist movement.[6] In this century, *Oroonoko* has been
reprinted four times, as part of Dobree's *Five Restoration Tragedies*
(1928), as a facsimile reprint of the 1739 edition (1969),[7] as an edition for the Regents Restoration drama series (1976), and, most
recently, as part of Sutherland's five-play anthology, *Restoration
Tragedies* (1977).

II *Southerne's Use of Sources*

The source of the tragic plot is well known: Aphra Behn's novel
Oroonoko, or, The Royal Slave, published in 1688, reprinted
throughout the eighteenth century and translated into several
languages. Although later generations knew Oroonoko primarily as
Southerne's character, the novel has long been regarded as, in
Summers's words, "indisputedly Mrs. Behn's masterpiece in
prose."[8] The novel is far more sweeping than the play, covering
Oroonoko's career as prince of Coromantien and general of the ar-
mies of his grandfather, the king. Both men fall in love with the
beautiful Imoinda, and the king, though impotent, forces her to
submit to him while Oroonoko languishes for love of her. Ultimately, through the conspiracy of a loyal servant, Aboan, and a cast-off
wife of the king, Oroonoko is able to consummate his secret
marriage to Imoinda. They are discovered, however, and while
Oroonoko is leading the army against invading enemies, she is sold
into slavery. Later he is told she is dead. Eventually Oroonoko, a
cultured prince who enjoys the company of Europeans, is lured onto
a slaving ship and betrayed into slavery, along with his retinue.

This is the point at which the play begins, the arrival and sale of Oroonoko and his company. Behn continues her story by introducing Trefry, an Englishman in Surinam who befriends Oroonoko and treats him as a special guest rather than a slave, in fact, keeping him from the company of slaves. Renamed Caesar, he is lionized by the society of the colony and displays his prowess when Indians attack and drive off Trefry's slaves. When he meets the much-talked-of Clemene, a beautiful slave, she turns out to be Imoinda. The reunion of the lovers begins a period of socializing which allows Behn to talk of Oroonoko's valor and great spirit; the narrator of the novel speaks in the first person as one who knew and sympathized with the black prince. But Imoinda is pregnant and her imminent delivery makes Oroonoko realize they are still slaves. He organizes the slaves to flee the plantations and set up a separate state, but they are pursued by the whites. When the others desert them, only Oroonoko, Imoinda, and a slave called Tuscan are left to fight. Eventually they are overcome and Oroonoko surrenders because the lieutenant governor, Byam, promises amnesty. But Oroonoko is seized and whipped, despite all Trefry can do. As overseer of the governor's plantation, to which Oroonoko belongs, Trefry is able temporarily to grant him some freedom of movement, but the continued slavery and despair of regaining freedom lead Oroonoko to kill Imoinda and her unborn baby. He intends to kill Byam and other enemies, and then kill himself, but grief over Imoinda weakens him and he is captured. At the end, stoically smoking a pipe, he endures the sequential dismemberment to which he has been sentenced for her death.

Southerne's retelling is far more compressed. Captured by the perfidy of Captain Driver, Oroonoko is given to Blanford, the representative of the absent Governor of Surinam. On his plantation Oroonoko is reunited with the pregnant Imoinda, his wife, the daughter of a European who had saved his life during a battle in his native Angola. For a time the reunited lovers enjoy the life of a prince and princess in exile, but Imoinda is the object of the lust of the lieutenant governor, and Aboan, Oroonoko's loyal servant, confined with the rest of the slaves, continually prods Oroonoko to take command of the slaves and do his duty as their prince. Oroonoko consents but Hottman, another slave, betrays him and his rebellion is quelled. In the fighting Captain Driver, the unscrupulous slave trader who tricked Oroonoko into slavery, is killed. Upon the lieutenant governor's promise of amnesty, Oroonoko surrenders, but he is immediately fallen upon, enchained, and separated from Imoinda. The lieutenant governor attempts to ravish her but she is rescued by Blanford, who has also released Oroonoko. As Imoinda flees in search of her husband, he is confronted by the dying Aboan, a victim of the tortures of the slavers, and gives him the dagger that allows him suicide. Together Imoinda and Oroonoko plan a joint suicide, and Imoinda's firm resolve brings about her death. Discovered by the parties of Blanford and the lieutenant governor, Oroonoko manages to kill his nemesis before killing himself.

To this action Southerne adds a comic plot, in which two sisters, unable to get husbands in London, turn in desperation to Surinam. Charlotte Welldon, disguised as a man and the brother of Lucy, wins the friendship of Stanmore, and the affection of the Widow Lackitt, who is resolved to marry her/him. Charlotte first marries off Lucy to the widow's "boobily son," Daniel, who enjoys the consummation but then rebels, until his mother and wife tame him. Charlotte pretends to marry the widow in secret but sends her longtime suitor, Stanmore's younger brother, Jack, to do the nightly duties. Stanmore is won by his affection for Welldon and the picture of Welldon's "cousin," Charlotte in female dress, to the extent that he hopes to marry her when she "arrives." Charlotte tests Stanmore as herself before revealing the hoax and letting him take her with no secrets. All of the principals of the comic plot are in sympathy with Blanford's party, Stanmore serving as an heroic adjunct to Blanford.

A number of conjectures have been made about the source of the comic plot, but none has been definitely proven. Romantic involvements in the colonies involving military figures, a widow, and persons fresh from London occur in Aphra Behn's *The Widow Ranter; or, The History of Bacon in Virginia*, produced posthumously in 1689; the title character and the tragic heroine both appear in men's clothing in the play. But the specific parallels are not strong, and we need only recall that the actress playing the breeches part here created the role of Sir Anthony Love (which also includes a mock marriage and husband-substitution) to realize that Southerne's own work provided ample precedent.[9]

While the play is chiefly derived from Behn's *Oroonoko* and Southerne's own imagination, there are overtones of *Othello* in the black-white marriage in the play, not surprising considering the extent to which Southerne was indebted to that play in earlier work. We see as well the heroic tones and tragic conflicts characteristic of "affective tragedy" at large.[10]

III   *The Theme and Power of* Oroonoko

Southerne's *Oroonoko* for a long time enjoyed popularity as a play about slavery. Alterations of the play usually attempted to make it more of an antislavery tract, while keeping the tragic tone uniform by excising the comic plot. Indeed, most of the critical writing not concerned with alteration has discussed the place of the play in the literature of the "noble savage."[11] Certainly much in the play warrants this kind of attention.

The basic conflict of the tragic plot is between the black slaves and the white plantation owners. Much of the sympathy for Oroonoko expressed throughout the play is devoted to antislavery speeches. The dread of slavery for his wife and child, the hopelessness of his condition, drives Oroonoko to his final fatal actions, but throughout the play the slavery system is soundly criticized. The blacks are continually betrayed and ill-treated; Aboan reports to Oroonoko:

> You do not know the heavy grievances,
> The toils, the labors, weary drudgeries
> Which they impose; burdens more fit for beasts,
> For senseless beasts to bear than thinking men.
> Then if you saw the bloody cruelties
> They execute on every slight offense,
> Nay, sometimes in their proud, insulting sport,
> How worse than dogs they lash their fellow creatures,
> Your heart would bleed for 'em.
>
>   (III, ii, 120 - 28)[12]

In the end Aboan himself comes to Oroonoko, fresh from beatings and tortures by the white men, and asks to die rather than to be a slave again.

The passion, the loyalty, the honor of Aboan is set against the cold-blooded, mercenary, dishonorable actions of such whites as Captain Driver, who announces how he traded on his friendship with Oroonoko to enslave him and receives the plaudits of the planters: "Such men as you are fit to be employed in public affairs. The Plantation will thrive by you" and "Industry should be encouraged" (I, ii, 173 - 75). The lieutenant governor is equally perfidious, unable to control his lust, and incapable of keeping his word to Oroonoko.

To some degree, though less than in Behn's novel, this conflict is also one between heathen and Christian, between a simple concept

of honor and devious hypocrisy. When Oroonoko chides the captain
for not keeping his word, he replies, "I am a better Christian, I
thank you, than to keep it with a Heathen" (I, ii, 196 - 97). Later
Oroonoko contemplates taking his revenge on the governor in kind:

> If I should turn his Christian arts on him,
> Promise him, speak him fair, flatter, and creep
> With fawning steps to get within his faith,
> I could betray him then as he has me.
>   (V, iii, 60 - 63)

Continually Oroonoko sees Christianity in the shape of those who
profess it most and follow it least, and his judgment of them is
tempered only by his friendship with Blanford, whose ideas of
righteousness and honor are so close to his own. When he realizes
that Blanford has rescued Imoinda from the lieutenant governor's
clutches, he says: "for his sake I'll think it possible / A Christian yet
may be an honest man" (V, v, 100 - 101).

Oroonoko's view of Christianity is one of the central concerns of
the play; continually he argues the untutored view of Christianity in
practice, rather than in theory. At the end of the play the uncom-
prehending Blanford, confronted with the fact of Imoinda's death
at Oroonoko's hand and the murder of the lieutenant governor,
pronounces a eulogy which contains an admonition to the audience:

> Pagan or unbeliever, yet he lived
> To all he knew; and if he went astray,
> There's mercy still above to set him right.
> But Christians guided by the heavenly ray
> Have no excuse if we mistake our way.
>   (V, v, 307 - 11)

In his view Oroonoko is absolved from guilt because while his sense
of honor or morality was not that of the Europeans, it was nonetheless a code by which he lived; the Englishmen of the play have
continually failed to live by the code to which they vocally ascribe.
In analyzing Oroonoko's sense of honor, we should not find it far
removed from that which animates principles governing heroic
figures throughout the age. A similar contrast animates the figure of
Montezuma in Dryden's *Indian Emperor* and even Almanzor in
The Conquest of Granada. As in so many other heroic dramas set in
exotic locales, the non-Christian values espoused are very like
idealized Christian values put into practice.

Moreover, for all the criticism of slavery implicit in the play, those critics who have treated the Oroonoko legend most thoroughly have continually pointed out that the play sometimes seems explicitly to condone slavery. Blanford after all, for all his virtues, seems unperturbed by the slavery of countless men, women, and children: "Most of 'em know no better; they were born so and only change their masters. But a prince, born only to command, betrayed and sold! My heart drops blood for him" (I, ii, 191ff.). As the play moved further into the era of the abolitionist movement, it seemed abhorrent that Oroonoko himself had sold slaves and that at one point he seems to justify the trade. Before Aboan persuades him, he rebels at the thought of having to murder "the innocent," the planters and slaveowners:

> If we are slaves, they did not make us slaves,
> But bought us in an honest way of trade
> As we have done before 'em, bought and sold
> Many a wretch and never thought it wrong.
> (III, ii, 107ff.)

He concludes that because the load is "so light" they "ought not to complain." It was to expunge speeches like this that alterations of the play were begun, and scenes added to heighten the horror of the audience toward the slave trade. The ultimate revision, *The Prince of Angola* by John Ferriar, so fully altered the play that the critic in the *Monthly Review* dismissed it as "avowedly a political pamphlet, and for that reason we do not consider it in a dramatic light."[13] Other critics have demonstrated that both Behn and Southerne were both presenting a hero so uncommon and removed from the general character of blacks in the story, like the cowardly slaves who desert Oroonoko in the midst of battle or the traitor, Hottman, as to seem utterly lacking in verisimilitude.

That criticism is undoubtedly correct if we assume that *Oroonoko* should be judged from the standpoint of the antislavery movement; however, several elements of the play mitigate against such a position. The first is the fact that the moral as pronounced by Blanford turns the play toward the audience and the society the audience represents. The implicit criticism is of English colonists and English manifestations of Christianity, just as Montesquieu's *Lettres Persanes* is about France, not the habits of Persians, and Swift's *Gulliver's Travels* is about the government of England and the society of man, not the island of Lilliput or the land of the

Houhnhnyms. To take Oroonoko as model of how to behave as a slave is to take Othello as a model of how to behave as a jealous husband or Romeo and Juliet as exempla of behavior for children of feuding families.

Second, we should recognize that even here Southerne does not discuss issues in black and white. The slavery question receives a full range of response: Lucy is wholly horrified; Blanford willing to accept it for others; the lieutenant governor torn by duty and lust; the planters, and especially Captain Driver, cruel and mercenary about it. Even the blacks have mixed responses: Hottman, for all his fiery denunciation of slavery, betrays the rebellion to the whites; the slaves at large are torn by terror of personal danger and desire for freedom; even Aboan, as passionate as he is in his persuasion of Oroonoko to revolt, is content to be Oroonoko's slave. Only Imoinda, possibly because she is a princess, continually is in abhorrence of slavery. Thus the full range of reactions is under analysis, and no one acts solely out of a full understanding of the implications of his actions—only the audience gains that insight.

This range is centered on the chief element of the play, the character of Oroonoko himself, and here is where Southerne's particular vision comes into play. The similarity with Othello is rather pronounced in several ways: like Othello, Southerne's Oroonoko has a white wife; like him, Oroonoko slays her and then wounds his chief oppressor before killing himself; and, finally, like Shakespeare's hero, Oroonoko is a man displaced in an alien culture. These similarities do not affect the play as markedly as they do in *The Disappointment*, where Shakespearean echoes determine the tone of the play; yet they do help us to see that Southerne's vision of Oroonoko is not primarily as a savage exemplum for civilized man or a symbol of the oppressions of slavery, however much such images may be implicit in the play, but as a tragic figure attempting to come to grips with the force of circumstances.

Like Antony in *All For Love*, Oroonoko is a man trying to do what is right but uncertain as to what that is. His sense of honorable conduct in the face of slavery is originally guided by his own experience of it and his ability to maintain a certain freedom in deference to his African rank and birth. His treatment has been different from that described as typical of slaves by Aboan; he is accorded many of the same privileges as a minor diplomat. He describes himself as "Favored in my own person, in my friends, / Indulged in all that can concern my care, / In my Imoinda's soft society" (III, ii, 142 - 46), and only gradually does he realize that his child and even Imoinda herself are in his own power only by his master's indulgence. The movement from passive slavery to open revolt is a process of educating Oroonoko to the full implications of the situation in which he exists. Like some anachronistic chivalric figure, he lives by a code of conduct which assumes too much honor and too much decency on the part of his captors. Instead of judging others by his own standards, he is forced to recognize that he is in the hands of men without the overwhelming sense of personal honor that governs his own behavior.

Unlike Othello, the tragedy of Oroonoko is caused not by his weakness from within but by his vulnerability from without. Like Aboan, who dies stoically, continually as Oroonoko calls him, "in life and death / The guardian of my honor!", Oroonoko and Imoinda are victims. In them Southerne again explores the psychology of the victim in the face of the brutishness of society. Preparing for suicide, Oroonoko laments, "The gods themselves conspire with faithless men to our destruction" (V, v, 132 - 33), and retreats from his fate in frantic imagining:

> O! that we could incorporate, be one,
> One body, as we have been long one mind.
> That blended so, we might together mix,
> And losing thus our beings to the world,
> Be only found to one another's joys.
>   (V, v, 211 - 15)

The long suicide scene continually works the audience's sympathies with the lovers to exact a full measure of affective response to their dilemma. Like Isabella's death, the deaths of Imoinda and Oroonoko, rather than being an indictment of their own weaknesses, are a condemnation of the exterior forces which narrow their options and leave them no choice but death.

IV *The Comic Plot*

Although critics of *Oroonoko* most often take to task the inclusion of a comic plot, as they did with *The Fatal Marriage*, Southerne's intention here as elsewhere is to provide a comic counterpoint to the tragic theme. Charlotte and Lucy Welldon are in their own ways equivalent to slaves in this society. Just as slaves are the commerce of the colony, mere chattel, so the women are treated like goods. In the opening speeches of the play, when Lucy complains that she thought "husbands grew in these plantations," Charlotte replies, "Why so they do, as thick as oranges, ripening one under another." Having left London because they were unable to arouse interest among its mén, they continually draw comparisons between a woman's fate and the lot of merchandise. Charlotte observes, "Women in London are like the rich silks; they are out of fashion a great while before they wear out—You may tumble 'em over and over at their first coming up and never disparage their price; but they fall upon wearing immediately, lower and lower in their value, till they come to the broker at last" (I, i, 23ff.). Later she says, "They say there is a vast stock of beauty in the nation, but a great part of it lies in unprofitable hands; therefore for the good of the public they would have a draft made once a quarter, send the decaying beauties for breeders into the country to make room for new faces to appear, to countenance the pleasures of the town" (I, i, 41 - 46). The strain of commercial talk continues when the widow Lackitt proclaims, "I have several stocks and plantations upon my hands, and other things to dispose of, which Mr. Welldon may have occasion for" (I, i, 216 - 18), and Stanmore urges Charlotte, disguised as Welldon, to marry the widow because of her estate, even though it crosses his own brother, Jack, who has pursued her but will "make nothing on it; she does not care for him" (I, i, 263). Throughout the opening scene of the play financial considerations and the metaphor of commerce dominate the dialogue.

The opening scene concludes with a preparation for the following scene and the introduction of the slave plot; Stanmore tells Charlotte that slavery is "the commodity we deal in, you know. If you have a curiosity to see our manner of marketing, I'll wait upon you" (I, i, 280 - 82). Almost immediately we return to the commercial language of the first scene, with complaints of the widow and the first planter about breeding the slaves; the planter asks Driver to "let the men and women be mingled together, for procreation sake, and the good of the plantation" (I, i, 14 - 16), and expects compliance because "I am a constant customer" (I, i, 21). The widow complains that "I am a woman myself and can't get my own slaves as some of my neighbors do" (I, ii, 12 - 13) and feels cheated that the prince has gone to another's lot, "set down to go as a common man" (I, ii, 47). If all this haggling were not by itself indicative of the parallels between plots, Charlotte makes them clear by interrupting the captain's negotiations for Lucy with the statement: "This is a market for slaves; my sister is a free woman and must not be disposed of in public" (I, ii, 126 - 27).

In the course of the play Lucy is wed to the widow's son, Daniel, a fool but a sharer in her estate; Charlotte herself holds out for Stanmore and uses the widow's desire for her as a man to provide Jack Stanmore, a younger brother and therefore not, like Stanmore, heir to an estate, with some financial security. Although Charlotte herself marries Stanmore under no constraints or trickery, the match is not really a triumph of romantic love, although it is more positive than the other two. The reward for her cunning is a mate worth the getting, but the cynicism of her world view has already been expressed in the play. She compares the double sexual standard to trade, noting that men can advance themselves by their sexual prowess while women are allowed one opportunity which they must make the best of for life. For the men,

theirs is a trading estate that lives upon credit and increases by removing it out of one bank into another. Now poor women have not these opportunities. We must keep our stocks dead by us at home to be ready for a purchase when it comes, a husband, let him be never so dear, and be glad of him; or venture our fortunes abroad on such rotten security that the principal and interest, nay, very often our persons, are in danger. If the women would agree (which they never will) to call home their effects, how many proper gentlemen would sneak into another way of living for want of being responsible in this? Then husbands would be cheaper.

(IV, i, 57 - 69)

This indictment of the double standard reminds us of the "hard condition of a woman's fate" which serves as an underlying motif in so much of Southerne's work. The comic plot ends as most do in Restoration plays, with the unjust world defeated; and then the play turns fully to the triumph of the unjust world in the tragic plot.

If the underplot seems sordid or distasteful to its critics, it is certainly not because Southerne was determined to play it safe with something for every one, high tragedy, sentimentality, farce, bawdry. The machinations of the mercenary interests of the comic plot are part and parcel of the world view held by the lieutenant governor, the captain, and most of the planters we see in the play. It indicts that society for hypocrisy in its own way. If the plight of Oroonoko and Imoinda seems to demean the comic plot by its intensity, that may not be altogether unlooked for: in *The Wives Ex-*

cuse and *The Maid's Last Prayer* Southerne's treatment of social norms in Restoration comedy had already reached toward bitter, almost tragic intensity; here that kind of comedy reinforces the indictment of the society at large.

V   *The Critical Reaction*

In the prologue to *The Spartan Dame*, Elijah Fenton wrote of Southerne that "His Oroonoko never fail'd to engage / The radiant Circles of the former Age." Together with *The Fatal Marriage*, *Oroonoko* settled Southerne's place in the affection of his audiences. *A Comparison between the Two Stages* claimed that *Oroonoko* was one of the three plays (the others were Vanbrugh's *Aesop* and *The Relapse*) that "subsisted *Drury-Lane* House, the first two or three years."[14] An early discussion of the Restoration theater, the *Comparison* suggests two of the typical responses to the play in this interchange between Sullen and Ramble:

S. *Oronoko!*
R. Oh! the Favourite of the Ladies.
S. It had indeed uncommon Success, and the Quality of both Sexes were very kind to the Play, and to the Poet: No Doubt it has merit, particularly the last Scene; but 'tis as certain, that the Comick Part is below that Author's usual genius.[15]

The success of the play was usually grounded in the power it had to move the emotions; Hawkesworth's revision grants this power in the prologue:

> This Night your tributary Tears we claim,
> For Scenes that *Southern* drew; a fav'rite Name!
> He touch'd your Fathers' Hearts with gen'rous Woe,
> And taught your Mothers' youthful Eyes to flow.[16]

This identification remains true to the end of the play's currency, and in fact grows stronger in the earlier eighteenth century with the abolitionist writers. In the novel *Slavery, or, The Times* (1793), the situation of a slave is highlighted by allusion to the play: "*Oronoko* was performed by command. My tears were the plaudits of a feeling heart."[17] The poem by Hannah More, "The Slave Trade," invokes Southerne as a muse:

> O. plaintive Southerne! whose impassion'd page
> Can melt the soul to grief, or raise to rage!
> Now, when the congenial themes engage the Muse,
> She burns to emulate thy generous views.

> No individual griefs my bosom melt,
> For millions feel what Oroonoko felt.[18]

But as much as the play was credited with the power to move audiences, it was criticized for its comic parts, with greater feeling as the play progressed through the eighteenth century into the nineteenth. Sullen's comment is mild compared to those that followed in the middle of the century. In the same prologue that praises Southerne, Hawkesworth complained:

> Yet, slave to custom in a laughing age,
> With ribald mirth he stain'd the sacred page;
> While virtue's shrine he rear'd, taught vice to mock
> And join'd in sport, the buskin and the sock.[19]

He called the comic scenes "some of the most loose and contemptible that have ever disgraced our language and theatre."[20] A reviewer of Hawkesworth's alterations agreed: "The tragic action was interrupted, not only by comic scenes, but by scenes of the lowest buffoonery, and the grossest indecency."[21] It became traditional to speak of revisions and alterations of the play in metallurgical terms, as Ferriar uses them: "lost in *Southern*'s dross, with clouded Ray, / Deform'd and rude, the Royal Image lay,"[22] or as Baker has it of Hawkesworth's version, "the Augean stable is indeed cleansed, the comic parts being very properly quite omitted."[23] Cumberland, preparing his own collection of the British drama, referred to the stage versions of the time as "cleanly" but his own, "the dirty copy of the author's work, as he originally published it."[24] In the same place he calls the appearance of the women of the comic plot, "an unaccountable prostitution of taste and character." Cumberland is generally severe with Southerne in either of his great tragedies, principally for unchristian behavior and general lowness of his characters. But the height of disapproval comes with William Archer, the most unsympathetic reader of Restoration drama of this century, who dismisses the play as "a

piece of unmitigated nonsense, in which a negro prince, freshly kid-
napped from Africa, talks fluent and bombastic blank verse, and is,
on the whole, an accomplished type of wishy-washy sentimental
heroism."[25]

But this strain of negativism is counteracted by the persistent
popularity of the play with audiences and recurring appreciation
even of its comedy. Genest wrote in 1832 that "it is the fashion to
abuse the Comic scenes—they are certainly very indecent, but they
have a great deal of the *vis comica* in them—in a moral light the
alterations of this play have been for the better, but in point of
dramatic merit vastly for the worse."[26] More recent critics have
amplified this general approval with the specific recognition of the
viability of the double plot play. Rothstein saw that "the subplot
about the husband-hunting of the Welldon sisters supports and
helps unify the tragic action," echoing themes from the tragic plot
in the comic "to achieve both grandeur and naturalness in his hero
and heroine."[27] Hume gives the comic portions even more importance, asserting that they provide "a necessary distraction from the
throbbing pathos of the central plot and gives us, once again, an example of Southerne's acute psychological perception and his ability
to clarify by contrast. Oroonoko's stature, the evil governor, and the
planters' avarice are simply part of a pathetic fairy story unless some
very everyday spectators are introduced for contrast."[28]

Like the argument about the comic plot, the debate about the
faithfulness of Southerne's depiction of slavery or the sincerity of his
opposition to it was essentially irrelevant to the artistic unity of the
play. As critics of the Victorian era continually shrank in horror at
Restoration bawdry, so critics of the abolitionist movement continually found the play wanting as a political tract. Hawkesworth's
revision, Gentleman's, the anonymous editor's of 1760, and especially Ferriar's recasting are essentially examples of the way men
will rewrite a play until it says what they want to hear. The chief
studies of the play in the traditions of the noble savage or the antislavery movement do little more than demonstrate that the
Oroonokos of Behn and Southerne, however much they inspire and
sustain more fully developed work in these traditions, are nonetheless separate from them. What all these interpretations fail to
recognize is the fact that the play sets out to be a tragedy and in this
light, it is, as Nicoll points out, "a decided triumph," for its great
sense of pathos, its portrait of Imoinda as "a frail flower bent by the
rude winds of civilized perversion and vice," and its fine cumulative

effect.[29] In some ways the contemporary view is coming back to that voiced by the earliest audience, particularly by John Oldmixon, who wrote that it was "written by Mr. *Southern*, with as much Purity and force, as any we have yet had from that Great Man. I cant say 'tis Regular enough, but had it been more correct, we should not easily have known which of Mr. *Otway*'s Plays to prefer before it."[30]

CHAPTER 8

The Last Plays

*O*ROONOKO, which insured Southerne's fame, seems to have helped secure him financially. At any rate, after its production and probably after his own marriage to a wealthy widow, he had no need to pursue his theatrical career. In fact, the prologue to *The Fate of Capua* suggests that Southerne had intended to stop writing:

> Our Bard resolv'd to quit this wicked Town,
> And all Poetick Offices lay down;
> But the weak Brother was drawn in again,
> And a cast Mistress tempted him to sin.

His theatrical involvement from the period after *Oroonoko* to the end of his life was to be intermittent and sporadic, occasional relapses of desire for a "cast mistress." In the thirty years between *Oroonoko* and the failure of his last play, Southerne produced only three plays. While these exhibit characteristic elements of his work, the gaps between them prevented the kind of intense development which had taken place between 1690 and 1696.

I   The Fate of Capua

In April of 1700 Southerne's *The Fate of Capua* was presented at Lincoln's Inn Fields by Betterton's company, with a strong cast that included Betterton as Virginius, Elizabeth Barry as Favonia, Verbruggen as Junius, and Bowman as Decius Magius.[1] John Downes, writing eight years later, said of it that it was "better to Read than Act: 'twas well Acted, but answer'd not the Companies Expectation."[2] What little evidence we have about the play seems to suggest that it failed on stage and was never revived beyond the initial performance. Southerne himself gives us no help: the play was printed without a preface, possibly a sign that Southerne saw no point in pursuing the issue.

Upon reading, it is difficult to know why the play failed, particularly if the performance was well done, since the play has a number of merits. It may be that audiences were unwilling to accept from Southerne a play which departed from the double plot formula of his previous success, for *The Fate of Capua* was wholly a tragedy, unrelieved by comic portions, and set not in contemporary foreign soil but in an Italian city during the Second Punic War. Southerne, however, was not inexperienced at writing tragedy in a classical setting; the incomplete *Spartan Dame*, and Dryden's *Cleomenes, the Spartan Hero*, which he helped complete, were both on classical subjects.[3] *The Fate of Capua* comes after a period of notable dramatic interest in such subjects. Southerne had provided the preface for Richard Norton's *Pausanias, the Betrayer of His Country*, published in 1696, a stage failure which, nonetheless, when taken with Hopkins's *Pyrrhus* (1695) and Gildon's *The Roman Bride's Revenge* (1696), suggests increasing support for the portrayal of what Hume calls the "classic-stoic mode," usually based on a story from classical literature or history and making overtures toward the French Neo-Classical stage.[4] *Pausanias*, Southerne tells us, was "built for the Experiment, upon the Model of the Antients, and according to the Reformation of the French Stage." Although that assertion is arguable, it does display interest and support for such plays. In the period following Norton's play, the classic-stoic mode produces Granville's *Heroick Love* (1698), Gildon's *Phaeton* (1698), Crowne's *Caligula* (1698), and Dennis's *Iphigenia* and Boyer's translation of Racine, *Achilles, or Iphigenia in Aulis* (both 1699). After Southerne, the classic-stoic mode continues intermittently to a peak with Addison's *Cato* (1713); in the main it does not produce a significant body of plays.

The Fate of Capua, Southerne's contribution to this mode, is a very serious attempt at high tragedy in the Classical tradition. Southerne found the story in Livy's *Roman History*, Books 23, 25, and 26, and in the main plot of the play his debt is very strong, with verbal parallels and direct inspiration apparent. His chief alterations are to confine the action solely to Capua, to transfer the speeches of some characters in Livy to main characters in the play, and to include the character of Decius Magius, who escaped to Rome by Livy's account, among those Capuan senators who prefer suicide to capture by the Roman forces.

The play centers upon questions of fidelity and faith. The Capuans, long allies of Rome, are persuaded by Pacuvius Calavius, one of their senators, to realign themselves with Carthage, whose

general, Hannibal, has won a major victory over the Romans.
Pacuvius's hope is that Capua will supplant Rome as the chief city
of Italy and that he himself will be its chief citizen. The motives of
ambition and powerlust in him are given support by a populace who
are unruly and vociferous, threatening the very lives of the senators
in their desire to align themselves with Hannibal. Pacuvius is able
to work the crowd much as Antony does in *Julius Caesar:* he at first
feigns a willingness to execute the senators which he then
counteracts by an insistence that each one be replaced by a better
man before he is executed; the crowd's inability to find better men
leaves the senate safe and indebted to Pacuvius. But the alliance
with Hannibal proves unwise from the beginning: first, Decius
Magius, the chief opposition to the Carthaginians, is arrested for his
views; then, the Carthaginians treat Capua like a conquered city,
ravishing its women and despoiling its wealth; and finally, Rome
rebounds to the attack, driving off Hannibal and turning the power
of its resources relentlessly toward revenge upon their former ally.
Certain of their own destruction, the senators are brought together
by Pacuvius for a final feast and mass suicide by poison, in which
they are joined by Decius Magius, the one man the Romans might
have let survive.

In this outline it is apparent that the conflict in the political plot
centers upon questions of loyalty. The argument among the
senators revolves around the clash between loyalty and expediency.
Pacuvius argues for expediency, the willingness to let old
allegiances crumble if they impede the rise of the Capuan state.
Livy says of him, "A bad man, but not utterly abandoned, he
preferred to dominate a state still intact rather than one that had
been wrecked."[5] On the other side, Decius Magius, to preserve ties
to Rome, argues past indebtedness, past loyalty, and shared origins
as peoples of Italy facing an alien invader. Most of his argument is
prompted by the speech in Livy to the Capuan legates by the
Roman consul, Varro.[6] Obviously Livy's bias is in favor of the
Roman side, and thus Southerne's Decius Magius, whose arrest by
Hannibal casts him in the role of righteous prophet, is the unregard-
ed voice of reason, proved right in the end.

In addition to the figure of Decius Magius, Pacuvius is opposed
by his son, Perolla, one of Magius's followers and a conspirator to
assassinate Hannibal.[7] The argument between father and son over
the plot centers on the conflict of loyalties again, the loyalty to the
state and the loyalty of a child to his parent. Perolla is dissuaded by

his sense of duty to his father, even though he knows the effect will
be disastrous:

> I must deny you nothing; but you have
> Undone your self, your Country, and your Son.
> You have commanded, and I will pay
> That Piety to you my Country claims.
>
> (308)

He here strikes again the note of portending doom already sounded
in the play by the mass murder of Roman citizens in bathhouses by
the Capuan crowds, the threat of mass murder of the senators, and
Magius's vow with Pacuvius that

> all that does belong to thee, and me,
> Our Children, Kindred, Family, and Name,
> May flourish, or decay, may rise, or rot;
> Be blest, or curst, as thou and I deserve
> From *Capua* and from the Commonwealth.
>
> (294 - 95)

So Perolla in bowing to his father bows to fate: "I can no more, but
with my Grief retire, / And in the Crowd expect the common Fate"
(308).[8]

The common fate reunites the opposing sides in Capua's quarrels.
In the end, Decius Magius, promised support by the Romans, rejects them to return to Capua, in order to tell the Senate of the
Roman sentence upon their state—to have its senators executed, its
noblest families exiled to other cities, its wealth confiscated, its
citizenry sold and removed, and the town itself given to "Slaves
made free, Strangers, and meanest Trades." He joins them in their
mass suicide for reasons of loyalty:

> what is Honour, Fortune, when we have
> No Friends, no Country, to rejoice with us?
> I could not think of Life after that Loss,
> Therefore came timely to prevent it here.
>
> (333)

Thus, despite his own innocence, Decius Magius remains loyal to
his own state, and shares its fate.[9]

Parallel to the political action of the play runs a love tragedy, for which no source is known to exist. But the elements of the action are familiar ones, in effect the same elements which animate *The Disappointment*. Here Virginius, husband of Pacuvius's daughter Favonia, is happy in his marriage, and saddened only by the loss of his dearest friend, Junius, in battle. Unknown to her husband or his friend, Favonia had loved Junius; and, when Junius is found among Capuan soldiers fighting for Rome and is paroled by the Carthaginians into Virginius's custody, we learn that he in turn had loved Favonia. Ill at ease in the house of the woman he loves and the friend he does not wish to betray, Junius peeks in on the sleeping Favonia as he takes his leave of the building. But Pacuvius and Virginius see him depart and assume that Favonia has been false. Husband and father both agree upon her death, but Virginius insists it be at her own hand, urging it on by such cruel treatment as displaying her child before her and then snatching it away. Eventually Favonia, offered a choice of a dagger or poison, drinks and dies. Virginius and Junius confront and fatally wound one another, Junius leaving evidence of her innocence before he dies.

The parallels between the plots are made pointed by the sequencing of the scenes. The triumph of Pacuvius and the happy prosperity of his plans is followed by the relief Favonia feels over the news of Junius's death, since she is no longer in danger of betraying the husband who brought them together. In the second act the premonition of doom for both plots begins with the coming of the Carthaginians and the injustice to Decius Magius and follows with the discovery of Junius and Virginius's insistence he come home with him. Favonia's metaphor for the calamitous situation she finds herself in foreshadows the fate of Capua itself:

> Let Blood, and Death, and Ruin be the Theme.
> Talk of the Massacres of Families,
> Plunder of Cities, and whole Countries waste.
> A private Mischief is not worth the News,
> Tell me that all the dire Calamities
> Of raging War, chain'd up in Discipline,
> Are now broke loose, trooping in horrid March,
> To fright the World, the Brood of *Cerebus*,
> And worry all, like the Black-guard of Hell.
> That Lust and Rapine do divide the Spoil:
> That Giant Murder does bestride our Streets,
> Stalking in State, and wading deep in Blood.
> My Father butcher'd, weltring in his Gore,

A Dagger in the Throat of my dear Child:
And thou shalt be as welcome then as now.

(301)

The invitation to Junius is a private catastrophe like the invitation to Hannibal on the political plane; Virginius, himself a supporter of Pacuvius, is like Pacuvius a man who has not considered the consequences of his actions. Just as Pacuvius sees the betrayal of the Romans as a stepping stone to power, Virginius sees the presence of Junius as a fulfillment of his own bliss, a reunion with his dearest friend, the man whom he describes as a rival to his wife who is in reality a rival to himself. In Act III the discovery of Carthaginian unreliability is followed by the discovery of Junius in Favonia's room; in Act IV the citizens are bombarded with news of Hannibal's reversals and the doom they must expect, and, immediately after, Favonia is harangued by her husband and given her options of death. In Act V Favonia, the innocent, dies, and the two men who had most interest in her, one wrong, the other ever true to her honor, die at her feet; in the same way, Pacuvius and Magius die together as their city dies. The double plot works in tandem throughout the play.

In a sense, despite its continual high seriousness and Roman setting, the elements of this play should be familiar to us from other Southerne plays. The love tragedy is once again a domestic drama, centered upon a wronged wife. Favonia, like Mrs. Friendall, is capable of feeling for a man not her husband and strong enough to resist it; here such resistance does no good. As in *The Disappointment* the relentless rage of the jealous husband is inexorable. We may even notice, in the use of verbal images of hell and death, echoes of Isabella, as we surely do in the onstage presence of the child before its mother. Favonia's lineage in Southerne's canon is clear, but the strength of her portrayal is not so great as in those other characters, possibly because there is less interaction among characters in this play and more reliance upon the emotional power of long speeches. Nor, we may add, is Virginius as strong a characterization as Alphonso or even Biron and Villeroy. Southerne avoids the temptation to borrow again from *Othello* and the strong passions of the jealous husband suffer from the lack of internal insight such as is offered in *The Disappointment*.

Another recurring element is the double plot, here effectively serious in both parts, unlike the underplots of the two great tragedies. Nonetheless the harmony of these plots is strong and consistent, contributing somewhat to the distance we feel from the characters at the same time it contributes to understanding the conflicts in either plot.

Finally there is the psychological element which one always finds in Southerne. The behavior of the principal figures in the main plot is complicated and multi-dimensional, as we expect: Decius Magius and Pacuvius are both complex figures, operating from a wealth of motives. Dodds complained that "Southerne's characterization of Pacuvius is uneven and relatively unsuccessful. He is perfidious, but in spite of his cold-blooded ambition there is an attempt made to draw sympathy to him."[10] But I rather think that he is multifaceted, as all men are, and that Southerne has once again not allowed us the luxury of lumping his characters into piles marked good and evil. Other figures of some complexity are Perolla, Favonia, Virginius, and Junius, all of whom act from motives often at war with other motives within them. Even the Capuan rabble, which in some ways demonstrates the persistent skepticism Restoration playwrights have of the popular voice, is consistently integrated into the fabric of the play, in ways it never is in *The Loyal Brother,* and reflects the complexity of the public view—distrust of government, susceptibility to demagoguery, understanding of events only when touched by them personally. All in all, it is, in Ward's words, "a fine blank-verse tragedy"[11] and, as Hume points out, "though over all it is too full of talk, it deserved better than its complete failure."[12]

II   The Spartan Dame

Thirty years elapsed between the time that *The Spartan Dame* was first begun and the time it first appeared on the stage of the Theatre Royal in Drury Lane, December 11, 1719. In some ways it seems to have been Southerne's special favorite among his plays, since he continually sought to have it performed; in the first edition of his *Works,* in 1713, he writes in the preface:

Eight Plays, I must own, are a numerous Issue for one Man to Father: And yet I have another, which I am told, might be pleaded in Abatement of the Faults of the rest, a Tragedy, call'd, *The Spartan Dame,* which I should have been glad to have seen among 'em for the Support of the Family; But she has not been allow'd to appear in Publick, even in the Person of Mrs. *Barry:* So wanting the Recommendation of the Stage, that Play is contented to lye by, and wait upon the Leisure of Peace, and the Humanity of the

Great Men in Power, to be permitted at one time or other to try its Fortune in the World.[13]

In his "Epistle to Mr. Southerne," prefixed to the 1713 collection, Fenton, as Southerne himself notes in the preface, praises the play highly, as a play that might restore the greatness of the tragic muse to the English stage:

> Perhaps the Beauties of thy *Spartan Dame*,
> Who (long defrauded of the Publick Fame)
> Shall, with Superior Majesty avow'd
> Shine like a Goddess breaking from a Cloud,
> Once more may reinstate her on the Stage,
> Her Action graceful, and Divine her Rage.[14]

When the play was finally published Southerne explained of its fortunes that the play "was begun a Year before the Revolution," and, "Many things interfering with those Times, I laid by what I had written for seventeen Years: I shew'd it then to the late Duke of Devonshire, who was in every regard a Judge; he told me, he saw no Reason why it might not have been acted the Year of the Revolution." Finishing it, he found objections to it still, until he had cut "very near the number of Four Hundred" lines.[15] Even at that it took the intervention of Congreve to win approval for its performance.[16] Finally, in the edition of the works of 1721 the four hundred lines were reinstated, although marked by quotation marks, and acknowledgment given to the Duke of Berwick, his military commander, for the original command to write the play and to John Stafford for having written the last scene of the third act.

In the same preface Southerne acknowledged that his publisher, Chetwood, had paid the extraordinary sum of £120 for the edited version.[17] Genest says of the profits on this play, "Southerne is said to have made £500 by this play—it was the practice formerly for an author to distribute tickets and solicit company to attend on his benefit nights—it was by this method that Southerne, who seems to have understood author-craft better than any of his contemporaries, made so much money of his plays."[18] Prior gives us evidence of this in a letter where he describes "Southern, my old acquaintance, having asked my assistance in getting him off with some tickets for his *Spartan Dame*," and elsewhere suggests that the play was satisfactorily received: "The *Spartan,* or, as they call it here, the *Smarting*

Dame has just done Tom S——'s business, and both he and the town are satisfied it has been acted, and are not troubled that it is laid aside."[19] Thus the life of Southerne's last tragedy seems to have been brief but profitable.[20]

The play itself is an interesting study in several ways. The political parallels which seemed so objectionable to so many for so long are apparent in the restored text. Most of the 400 lines deal with topics of loyalty to a king in terms equivalent to a defense of James II; almost all these lines are from the political plot, where the old king, Leonidas, is deposed by a popular revolution which brings in his daughter, Celona, and her husband, Cleombrotus, in his stead. The correlations in James II, Mary II, and William III are obvious, and the pleas by Southerne and Congreve that the play is not inflammatory to the Jacobite cause—England and France were continually at war and the Jacobites began a rebellion in 1715 and again in 1745—are somewhat disingenuous. Southerne's play is totally in sympathy with the cause of the overthrown king and against the view of the crowd and the forces of usurpation, all of whom act for dishonorable motives of greed, ambition, and lust.

In fact, Southerne considerably alters the view of his acknowledged source toward the characters to present the view he does. In Plutarch's life of Agis, Leonidas, the king whose place is usurped by Cleombrotus, is viewed as a man opposed to reform, a man serving special interests, who impedes the return of Sparta to her ancient honesty and selflessness. Cleombrotus, his son-in-law, is primarily a tool of reform forces, led by Agis, whom Leonidas cruelly suppresses. Only his relationship with Leonidas's daughter saves Cleombrotus from the fate of Agis and the others, assassination or banishment; and he is allowed to live with his wife in retirement from public life. Plutarch's sympathies are clearly with the man Cleombrotus supports, Agis, and Cleomenes, the subject of the succeeding biography, who was inspired by Agis in the cause of reform. But Southerne ignores Plutarch's assessment of Leonidas and deepens the villainy of Cleombrotus.

The removal of the lines specifically pointing to the parallels with the historical situation may in some way explain the apparently warm reception of the play, since when that overlay is removed, it is a busy tragedy with virtually no political dimensions at all. Actions of state and private actions are seen at the same level and the plot turns, as *The Loyal Brother* did, more on personal behavior than public. Once Leonidas has been deposed, Cleombrotus is free to ignore his wife Cleona and pursue his desire for Thelamia, her sister, wife to Eurytion, loyal supporter of Leonidas. Thus, a large part of the play deals with the machinations of Crites, the double agent, to win Cleombrotus a place in Thelamia's bed. He eventually does this by feigning to her that her husband has secretly returned, but after consummation she discovers the trick and the tyranny of Cleombrotus is exposed. Moreover, Cleombrotus's lust has made him ignore Crites's hopes to kill Leonidas and secure the throne that way; Thelamia's betrayal merely gives the opposition a further cause for revolution.

The focus here is on the suffering of the two sisters: Celona is torn between loyalty to her father and loyalty to her husband, and even when she moves to persuade the people to restore her father, she does so not completely against her husband's interests. At the end, she argues that she could not assassinate him, as Leonidas has been led to believe she might, because she owes him her loyalty as a wife; later, even after she knows he has ravished Thelamia, she pleads for his life. No guilt attaches itself to her, and, after Cleombrotus is killed by Eurytion, she resolves to retire from the world.

In counterpoint to her is Thelamia, a loyal wife betrayed by her friends, whose case is strikingly likened to and foreshadowed by her reading of the rape of Lucrece by Tarquinus, a story traditionally well known and the subject previously of *Lucius Junius Brutus, The Father of His Country*, a play by Nathaniel Lee which bears many resemblances to this one, particularly in the ties between political tyranny and sexual aggression. At the same time, her plight is like that of Monimia in *The Orphan* or even Isabella's, a woman despoiled through the machinations of men and obliged to die because dishonored.[21] In either way of viewing her, we have a strong portrait, but the play never fully lives up to the promise of these contrasts of suffering sisterhood.

Partly this is because the male characters are one-dimensional. Leonidas has several affecting moments as the father attempting to decide between the state and the life and honor of his third daughter, the virginal Euphemia, whom Cleombrotus threatens to have raped by slaves and murdered, or as the king willing to remain without his throne rather than use dishonorable means to restore it. Cleombrotus is chiefly villainous and Eurytion chiefly virtuous. Crites has some life as a Iago-like figure—his wife's relationship with Thelamia is similar to that of Emilia's with Desdemona in *Othello*—and he is in some ways the play's most complex character,

but he too is mainly villainous. While the tragedy has some affective moments, then, on the whole it is not the equal of the other
tragedies by Southerne.

In part the failure of the play is in its blurred vision. An example
is the characterization of Euphemia. Not a character in Plutarch,
Euphemia seems to have been added as an allegorical figure for
Queen Anne, the younger daughter of James II, whose reign might
have been seen by Southerne as a reconciliation of the opposing
parties in England. At the end of the play, she is given an en-
comium which suggests that the high hopes being showered on her
are allegorical, since they in no way suit the context of the play.
Thus the paean to Euphemia sounds hollow, because the political
nature of the play is not harmonized with its personal nature. After
the stereotypical villainy of his life, Cleombrotus dies wordlessly at
Eurytion's hand and Thelamia's suicide by poison, while inevitable,
is almost an afterthought in the bustle of the finale; neither is a
significant action with repercussions beyond the events themselves.
Celona's praise of Euphemia focuses the attention of the conclusion
on a character who has had the least to do with the progress of the
play; consequently, attention is drawn from the personal tragedies
of Celona, whose widowhood impells her to a nunnery, and
Thelamia, who is led offstage by Eurytion to die, and also from the
political implications of the restoration of Leonidas to the throne.
Nor does the triumph of the righteous have any moral force: Crites
is already dead, killed by Cleombrotus (who had been tricked into
believing Crites's men allowed the entrance of Eurytion's troops
into the besieged city); the death of Cleombrotus himself, considering his importance as a villainous figure who has caused so
much havoc in the play, is very understated.

Thus *The Spartan Dame* never achieves the power of Lee's
Lucius Junius Brutus as a play of ideas and political significance;
nor can it rival, on the other hand, the force of Southerne's own *The
Fatal Marriage* as a domestic tragedy. As a merger of domestic and
political ideas, both *Oroonoko* and *The Fate of Capua* are far
superior. It shows us, nonetheless, both the same interest in the
plight of oppressed womanhood that the comedies and tragedies to
succeed it showed and the stylistic hallmarks of the early plays, particularly the close relationship between short speeches and the frequent ending of one character's thoughts in the words of another.

Genest said of it that some parts "have great merit, but on the
whole it is far from a capital play," and that assessment is just. But

he was off target when he complained that "Southerne should have studied Plutarch's life of Lycurgus, when he sat down to write this play, for want of doing so, he betrays much ignorance of Spartan manners."[22] In the main, the anachronisms he cites are not the play's chief defects; in fact Crites's mention to Thelamia of men who railed at marriage is a cunning piece of psychology in which he attempts to persuade her of the propriety of infidelity without actually seeming to argue for it, and the story of Lucrece, while of course historically later than the events of the play, is nonetheless an effective foreshadowing of the coming fate of Thelamia and an analogy providing powerful reverberations throughout the play.

It is on this level of momentary effectiveness that the play's chief virtues lie. As Dodds observes, "the stage success of Southerne's tragedies depended more on theatrically effective situations than on well-wrought plots."[23] Such moments are Thelamia's reading of the story of Lucrece or her scene with Celona describing the rape, or the scenes in which Leonidas struggles with conflicting impulses. But such scenes do not carry the play in ways his earlier plays were carried; and, after an initial run of nine days, sufficient to make Southerne a handsome profit, the play received scant attention.

III   Money the Mistress

From the beginning *Money the Mistress* seemed doomed to failure. William Broome, who had once sent Southerne a complimentary poem to win his favor, learned from Elijah Fenton that the play had been rejected at Drury Lane and was taken to the other house; patronizingly Broome wrote Pope:

Mr. Southerne wants an epilogue, and will oblige me to write it. I am sorry he brings his play on the stage. His bays are withered with extreme age. From what I heard of it with you at Sir Clement Cottrell's, it cannot bear water, and the lead of my epilogue, fastened to the end of it will add to its alacrity in sinking. Mr. Southerne's fire is abated, and no wonder when philosophers tell us that the warmth and glory of the sun abates by age. It requires some skill to know when to leave off writing.[24]

Fenton claimed that "I have not seen above two scenes of his comedy, in which I find the old man was too visible."[25] Even the prologue by Leonard Welsted pleaded for audience leniency because of Southerne's age:

> O! then protect, in his declining year,
> The man, that fill'd your mothers' eyes with tears!
> The last of Charles' bards! The living name,
> That rose, in that Augustan age, to fame.

It would seem that everyone was prepared for failure, and not surprisingly, it came.

At its premiere on January 19, 1726, at Lincoln's Inn Fields, the play was soundly hissed. Benjamin Victor writes:

I happened to be behind the Scenes the first Night of this Comedy, and was very sorry to find that the Audience did not take the Age, as well as the great Merit of this Author, into their Consideration, and quietly dismiss this last weak Effort to please them. When they were hissing dreadfully in the fifth Act, Mr. *Rich*, who was standing by Mr. *Southern*, asked him, if he heard what the Audience were doing? His Answer was, "No, Sir, I am very deaf."[26]

The play was performed only three times, up through the author's benefit night, and then withdrawn. But the spirit of condescension toward the play has persisted since that time.

It really is not as bad as all that. Genest writes, with some justice, that "it is a tolerably good piece, and by no means a proof that the author's faculties were impaired by age, as has been said."[27] Most of Southerne's own defense of the play, in the dedication, is apt. He writes:

If the tale be good, the plot well laid, and digested into the strength and support of the whole; the disposition of the business natural and easy; the incidents proper and prepared; the sentiments honourable and virtuous, and the writing able to speak for itself, all which I hope I have secured in this piece, I shall think that I have done my part: It is framed on the model of *Terence*, and as comedies ought to be, not to do harm; the characters in nature, the manners instructive of youth, and at least becoming sixty and six, the age of the writer. I have punished infidelity in the lover, and falseness in the friend. (176)

By his own lights Southerne pretty well achieved what he set out to provide.

Even without the dedication we could see Southerne's intention clearly by the nature of the changes he rings on this source material. In the Comtesse Marie d'Aulnoy's *Ingenious and Diverting Letters of the Lady* ——*Travels into Spain*, the story is quite a bit harsher.

There, Mariana, the widowed Marchioness de los Rios, tells how she had two suitors before her marriage. She initially had refused the rich and honorable Marquess de los Rios, because of the differences in their ages, and much preferred Mendez, a merchant's son. When Mendez is captured by Algerian pirates and held for ransom by Meluza the Corsary, the Marquess decides to marry Mariana in spite of her preferences, since he has the approval of her father, Davila. In response, Mariana and her friend Donna Henrietta take de los Rios's gift of jewels to ransom Mendez, but the jewels disappear and Mariana is forced to stand for surety that Mendez will return with his own ransom. When Mendez and Henrietta do not return, it is only after two years that Mariana learns that they have not been lost at sea, but are married and living in Seville. Mariana writes her father and is ransomed by the Marquess, whom she marries out of gratitude. In two years he dies and she again meets Mendez, himself a widower; feeling her old attraction for him she retreats to a religious life at Burges, rather than follow her desires.[28]

In Madame d'Aulnoy it is a somber story of betrayed love and the weaknesses of a woman's emotions; but in Southerne the story is altered to point to a moral about mercenary motives and physical attractiveness. Mariana is drawn to Mourville, a young, handsome French lieutenant-colonel at Tangier. His rival is Colonel Warcourt, an older Englishman, the choice of Mariana's father. Warcourt, however, defers to Mariana's preference rather than use his power with her father to marry her against her will. When Mourville sets out against the Moors and, in exceeding his orders for a display of valor, is captured by Moluza, the Governor of Tangier refuses to ransom him. Mariana's father, Davila, is sent as a negotiator to the Moors' camp, accompanied by Mariana and Harriet, disguised and veiled to hide their identities from Davila, whom they have bribed to take them along. At first Mourville is jealous of Warcourt and possessive of Mariana, but once she has stayed behind and he and Harriet have left the camp to seek the ransom money, Harriet persuades him that Mariana's father has been ruined by a ship disaster and that Mourville should marry her, because she herself is rich. In fact, Harriet pawns the jewels given by Warcourt as a gift to Mariana and later we learn that the disaster at sea ruined her family, not Davila. Eventually Warcourt rescues Mariana and the perfidy of Mourville and Harriet is exposed and condemned; both the Governor and her father urge Mariana to marry Warcourt, but the play ends with her hesitant and in need of time to think.

Southerne's version of the story does not go nearly as far as Madame d'Aulnoy's, partly because, while she is interested in writing a romance, he is interested in producing an exemplum. The whole of the play is directed toward the punishment of those who place money before love and the education of those who cannot tell superficial luster from real merit. Thus the character of Mourville is portrayed as contradictory in nature: he attacks Warcourt for his wealth, and suspects Mariana of deserting him for money—"When I remember how many women have unblest the ordinance of a marriage, by a prostitution of bed and board to old age, infamy, deformity, and disease . . . I cannot but wonder at the bewitching charm of money; and believe it difficult to be overpowered when it is presented by a valuable hand" (198); yet he abandons Mariana for Harriet, of whom he had never thought, once he is convinced Mariana is penniless—"I own she was not the less handsome for being the daughter to a rich man" (216). In the end he is guilt-ridden and tied to a penniless and deceitful wife, and Harriet is publicly exposed as a cheat and a liar. Just as Mourville falls in part by adapting the way of the world he earlier had opposed, Harriet is the ironic embodiment of her own argument to Mourville: "Beauty may charm you to a marry'd life / But sense and conduct join to make the wife" (218).

In a sense Mourville and Harriet have been painfully educated; equally painful is the education of Davila and Mariana. In spite of her preferences, Davila had urged Warcourt upon Mariana because of his wealth and merit; and his mercenary interests are further revealed when he takes money from the disguised young women to take them to the Moorish camp and hints that he might have sold them as slaves had they not told him their "father" was Benzaddi, the rich Jew. When he learns that she is a prisoner and believes himself destitute, he comes to some sense of his own folly, admitting "by our severity, or fondness, fathers are commonly fools" and that "the love of money" had impelled him to force the issue between Mourville and Warcourt. But Mariana is the greatest learner of the play and her lesson is that the merit of a man may rest not in his youth, gallantry, or good looks, but in his virtue, honor, and compassion. At the end of the play she is humbled and contrite, and Warcourt alone in the play seems to have deserved good fortune.

The Governor announces the moral of the play:

> These patterns lay before our female youth,
> The sure effects of gallantry, and truth.
> If from their parents' care they wildly run,
> They see the ready road to be undone.
> But if they wou'd secure content for life,
> A prudent choice must make the happy wife.
>
> (241)

The pietistic tone of the play is very pronounced throughout, and although the closing lines are reminiscent of the ending of *The Fatal Marriage* in their sententious moralizing, the earlier play was in no way so obvious or so single-minded. Even the subplot of *Money the Mistress* is nothing more than a brief exemplum. A Spaniard, Manuel, pays court to Diana, the wife of the French officer, Marsan, and only comes to learn a lesson when Marsan turns the tables on him and courts Teresa, Manuel's wife, in return. Thus the whole tone of the play is reforming and didactic.

Much of what is wrong with the play stems from this tone. A good many speeches are static and pompous, filled with sermonizing rather than dramatic significance. As a consequence many of the characters are underdeveloped and predictable; most of the prospects for introspection of complex characters are either overstated or underplayed, with no characters complexly delineated; and the behavior of each only serves to reinforce a moral rather than examine one.

Dodd felt that "at the end of his long dramatic career Southerne was embracing, albeit somewhat gingerly, the Sentimental Muse. There is evidence in his earlier work to show that the transition is no surprising one."[29] At heart, of course, Southerne had always been a moralist—his target for satire had been the mercenary nature of marriage and the predatory conduct of men in his three earlier comedies—and he had always had compassion for women in distress. In this sense Mariana is the last of a long line extending from Semanthe in *The Loyal Brother*. The comedies are very serious in their motives and the tragedies usually take the side of the innocent against a foolish or vicious society. But here the target is rather obvious and the treatment without the fire or the power—even in brief scenes—of the earlier plays. Clearly the Terence upon which this play is modeled is not that which Dryden recommended in the dedication to *The Wives Excuse*.

CHAPTER 9

Conclusion

REFERENCES to Thomas Southerne in his lifetime are plentiful but usually brief. The picture that emerges from what amount to little more than footnotes to other men's lives is that of a well-fed, jovial companion and guest. Except for some back-biting by such a figure as William Broome, the references are always affectionate, cheerful, good-natured. He is teased about his deafness, asked after by corresponding friends, and applauded for his graciousness and generosity. In all this welter of reference, there is surprisingly little mention of his work, either positively or negatively. It is as if the man's personality and social grace had completely effaced the accomplishment of his literary career. And, indeed, the references to him in the close of his life as "the poet's Nestor" or "great Otway's peer and greater Dryden's friend" seem to suggest that it was as much longevity as talent, as much nostalgia for the era in which he wrote as the plays he created, that elicits respect and regard.

We can judge from such evidence that Southerne was one of those men whose character is so evenhanded and unassuming that he seldom inspires either great enmity or great admiration. And, in fact, Southerne is attacked personally in the period only over the question of his political loyalties. Even then, the attacks are mild and factional and create no significant controversy.[1]

In the same way, the references to Southerne's work, while often laudatory, strangely lack the depth and breadth of attention given to that of his contemporaries and friends, such as Dryden, Otway, Congreve, and Vanbrugh. The opposition to the "blasphemy" and "obscenity" of the stage, while pummeling Congreve and Vanbrugh, two men much akin to Southerne in their work, seldom gives him more than a passing slap. And while his tragedies are sometimes mentioned in the same breath with those of Shakespeare, Otway, and Lee, critical attention, even by such a friend as John Dennis and a contemporary as Charles Gildon, is never focused on

118

his work. Nonetheless the passing references have in some ways
determined the nature of critical responses to his work right up to
this century. Now, as Southerne edges his way into the select circle
of Restoration authors for whom there is continuous critical attention, we need to reevaluate carefully his accomplishments and what
they mean in terms of Restoration and eighteenth-century theater.

I   *The Accomplishment of Thomas Southerne*

Surveying Southerne's career, Dodds charged that "politically
and professionally he was an opportunist."[2] In his view, "by 1695
Southerne had written five plays, all stamped with the formula of
lubricous wit. It was the fashion";[3] however, he continues, Collier's
attack on the theater led to reform on the stage and in Southerne's
writing, as shown by the exemplary *Money the Mistress*. He further
argues that "a survey of his plays in chronological order would show
his progressive attempt to adjust his methods to popular demand."[4]
There are, however, a number of reservations we might have about
this judgment.

First of all, the matter of Southerne's financial success in the
theater seems to trouble certain critics—one biographer sneered
that he "was not beneath the Drudgery of Sollicitation . . . which,
perhaps, *Dryden* thought was much beneath the Dignity of a
Poet."[5] But surely popular success carries no certain onus with
it—witness Shakespeare and Dickens. Second, the theatrical and
cultural context of Southerne's work needs to be considered before
we dismiss his changes of genre and mode as commercial self-
serving—again we have the range of Shakespeare's work before us;
indeed, most of the chief seventeenth-century dramatists produced
plays of considerable variety. The failure or inability to adapt to
changing times or to avoid stale repetition has often signaled the
end of literary careers. But the most important reason to distrust
Dodds's assessment is simply that a survey of Southerne's plays in
chronological order shows a certain unity of theme and design in his
works and a fairly consistent and conscientious world view being expressed.

At the heart of his earliest play, *The Loyal Brother*, Southerne is
interested in the analysis of character in reaction to a crisis chiefly
envisioned as domestic. Although such an examination of conflicting motives has its roots in the origins of heroic drama generally, especially the love-and-honor plays of the reign of Charles I,

Southerne's focus is closer to the pathetic tragedy of Dryden (in *All For Love*), Otway, Banks, and Lee. We see this in his attempts to render the complicated motives of most of his characters, but primarily in the analyses of themselves and their situations by Tachmas, Seliman, and Semanthe.

It becomes clearer in *The Disappointment*, where the attention of the play is freed from the encumbrance of the political allegory and the state plot, and where Southerne establishes a second hallmark for his plays, the panorama of motivation. Here the main crisis is similar to that of *The Loyal Brother*, the threat to a good woman's virtue; but Southerne has heightened it by domesticating it, focusing on a distressed wife and her obsessively jealous husband, and broadening the context to include a set of characters who provide a range of responses to questions of sexual intrigue. Southerne's lack of sympathy with the libertine world view is pretty clearly expressed here, and that attitude will remain consistent throughout his work. Finally, *The Disappointment* demonstrates Southerne's seriousness of intention by its verbal echoes of several of Shakespeare's plays, revealing not only his indebtedness but the degree to which he saw himself working in a tradition of high moral and artistic design.

In effect, Southerne, particularly in *The Disappointment*, is working independently of stage tradition even at the moment he seems so overwhelmed by a potpourri of influences and conventions. While he relies on conventions to express certain kinds of characters or situations, his response is usually unconventional—he sees tragic intensity in conventions usually reserved for comedy, particularly in the later comedies. The effect of his use of conventions is to subvert them and, thus, to subvert the social tradition or ethic which they represent.

If we place *The Spartan Dame* in its proper chronology we do not see a development expressly from *The Disappointment* except that here Southerne is able to free himself from his reliance upon earlier models; the play does, however, offer clear equivalences to Lee's *Lucius Junius Brutus*. There is also greater control of the tendency, derived from Restoration tragedy, to develop powerful moments at the expense of overall design. The play's greater unity tightens the relationship between public and private plots and the analysis of motive and the development of character is far less bombastic and overt than in his earlier plays. Yet, partly perhaps because the play was virtually commissioned rather than inspired by the playwright himself, the play is not nearly as dynamic and forceful as the earlier two.

With *Sir Anthony Love* Southerne tries the fourth kind of drama in four plays, comedy, and succeeds remarkably well. Yet in some ways this is experimental work of the order of the earliest plays, not completely coherent, sometimes labored and self-conscious, but generally successful as a potent and consistent work. We see here, in the adaptation of an Aphra Behn story, Southerne's ability to transform material to fit a unified structure and to see as well the levels of interrelationships revolving around a central theme or character—here Sir Anthony / Lucia—which is the kind of unity found in his best plays. Although in many ways it is a very successful play, it lacks the power its design portends—one feels that what was meant to be ironic and subversive too often seems either overstated or ambiguous—and ultimately dissipates its vision in overextended banter.

Particularly in *The Disappointment* and *Sir Anthony Love* Southerne has fashioned extremely interesting and provocative near-successes, and all the first four plays demonstrate clearly derivative but nonetheless distinctive talents. But *Sir Anthony Love*, perhaps because of its success, is tantamount to a final rite of passage before emergence into acknowledged artistry. The four plays which follow, each in its own way, display the unique properties of Southerne's talent in highly effective and memorable ways.

The Wives Excuse offers a singular vision of the free-gallantry ethic in contemporary society. Its focus is wholly domestic and contemporary, centered upon a distressed heroine, Mrs. Friendall, whose situation is recounted with compassion but without maudlin sentimentality. Its revelation of a continuum of male predators and female victims includes several striking portraits of complicated and uniquely motivated characters to whom the audience must often have conflicting responses. It raises the comic conventions to near-tragic intensity and tends to subvert them thoroughly. In addition to several telling dialogues and soliloquies, Southerne includes the innovations of attention chiefly to a married couple, an opening scene in which secondary, low characters delineate the primary characters, and the presence of an author-surrogate who discusses the departure from convention in the play itself. Overall it is a masterful work, poignant and powerful, superbly designed and executed.

The Maids Last Prayer is equally powerful but its impact is the reverse of *The Wives Excuse*. It too focuses on marriage, offering a range of responses; it too argues against self-serving and hypocrisy in sexual relationships; but its range of characters is darkly satiric, savaging the conventions of libertine comedy rather than subtly undercutting them. Its brutal force derives chiefly from a series of self-portraits in soliloquy by the central characters which pinpoint their locations on a chart of a social wilderness.

Artistically these two comedies are Southerne's triumphs: *The Wives Excuse* rivals the best of Congreve's plays, and *The Maid's Last Prayer*, the angriest of Wycherley's. Both stand apart from the double tradition of hard and humane comedy (in Hume's terms), and strike a middle position indicative of the best plays of the period to follow. They were succeeded by Southerne's greatest commercial triumphs, both of which carry on the principles of composition and structure developed in the comedies.

The Fatal Marriage, by its focus on a distressed heroine, its range of characterizations, and its parallel plotting, is linked to both *The Disappointment* and *The Wives Excuse*. As he had darkened the prospects for his heroine in Mrs. Friendall's plight, Southerne carried the beleaguered Isabella to ultimate destruction, protesting the ways of the world regarding marriage and women's freedom. The play is solid and unified, even with the balance of comic and tragic plots, and its analysis of character thorough and disturbing.

Oroonoko is similarly constructed, but its vision is even darker and more distressing, since it aligns an essentially heroic tragedy with intrigue comedy, the slavery of men with slavery of women. On one level, then, the play is part of a consistent vision—not merely the theatrical interest in the distress of a female but a philosophical and social concern over the exploitation of women. On another level, Oroonoko himself is another of Southerne's portraits of a man struggling to make sense out of his circumstances, as Tachmas does in a tentative way in *The Loyal Brother* or as Alphonso does in *The Disappointment*. Again we have the range of responses to conditions, here the issue of slavery. The unity of the play allows a powerful reaction to the condition and fate of its protagonists. In this play, as in its predecessors, Southerne has learned to push on into tragedy, using tragic conventions, to win an audience to a tacit acceptance of his thesis, rather than violate convention and lose his audience. There is still subversion in the underplot of *Oroonoko* but its very ability to sustain itself as a comic action is what caused its abandonment years later.

As we have seen, the two tragedies held the stage for a long time, some demonstration of Southerne's success in their construction, and the chief characters, Isabella and Oroonoko, became household words. In *The Fate of Capua* we see Southerne's most successful political play, on the theme of loyalty, which owes its artistic success, though commercially it failed, to the complete integration of political and private plots. The play is far more universal in design than *The Loyal Brother* or *The Spartan Dame*, far less limited to its political circumstances, and its impact less controversial because not clearly of current significance. Nonetheless it shows a falling off of power, a reworking of familiar themes—the distressed wife and unjust husband, the range of male reactions to a woman's condition—which here never reach the intensity of the earlier tragedies. It is as if Southerne had lost the spontaneous power of his earlier plays in seeking after the unity of tone and mood he achieved in his last tragedy. Still, it is a readable and well-wrought play, and its analysis of complex motives in the political characters is telling and significant.

It hardly seems fair to hold Southerne to account for *Money the Mistress* after twenty-six years of absence from dramatic writing. While it is an interesting play, it is too pat—a condition not simply of the time in which it was written, but of the tendency in Southerne to unity which here simply becomes too mechanical. The heat and force of the four chief plays are missing, and an exemplum told with a certain amount of smugness is offered in their place.

What then is the accomplishment of Thomas Southerne in these plays? When we strip away the apprentice work and the final plays, we are left with a core of drama rivaling, although not always equaling, the best of its period. Southerne changes the emphasis in comedy to the married couple, provides stunning psychological portraits of the social types of his time, writes two of the most compelling comedies of the era, helps develop the pathetic tragedy and advance the emphasis on domestic concerns, and establishes four tightly unified plays exploring, from a variety of perspectives, the central issue of Restoration comedy: the problems of marriage.

II *The Influence of Thomas Southerne*

Thomas Southerne's personal accomplishment was significant—the growing range of critical acclaim attests to that. It is more difficult to gauge his accomplishment in terms of its impact on

the theater. Surely there was continual acknowledgment in his own
time that his place ought to be high. Buckinghamshire pictured in
"The Election of a Poet Laureat" (1719):

> Apollo, now driven to a cursed quandry,
> Was wishing for Swift, or the fain'd Lady Mary:
> Nay, had honest Tom Southerne but been within call—.[6]

In "A New Session of the Poets, Occasion'd by the Death of Mr.
John Dryden," Kenrick wrote to Congreve, "You write correct, but
Southerne writes as well," and then wrote:

> Next Southern to the Judge himself apply'd,
> With haughty Oroonoko by his Side;
> The Ladies pity, and the Author's Pride.
> Southerne, who still shew'd Nature on the Stage,
> Not whines his Tender, nor too rough his Rage.
> Apollo told him he deserv'd the Bays,
> Had he been contented to write three Plays.—
> But since he knew not when he Glory won,
> 'Twas just, that *Capua*'s Fate should be his own.[7]

These views of Southerne take his talent as a matter of course and
the judgment of Kenrick is close to that held throughout the tenure
of the two tragedies upon the stage. Hazlitt wrote in 1814 that he
had "wept outright" during Sarah Siddons's performances as
Isabella, and "this we take to have been a higher employment of
the critical faculties than doubling down the book in dog-ears to
make out a regular list of critical common-places." Elsewhere he
wrote of the eighteenth century that no play in it could "be read
with any degree of interest or even patience, by a modern reader of
poetry, if we except the productions of Southern, Lillo, and Moore,
the authors of The Gamester, Oroonoko, and Fatal Curiosity, and
who instead of mounting on classic stilts and making rhetorical
flourishes, went out of the established road to seek for truth and
nature and effect in the commonest life and lowest situations."[8]

The feeling for Southerne's place among his contemporaries, as
"great Otway's peer," was largely founded on his ability to wring
the passions, as Otway had done, and to use language that seemed
right for the situation and the theatrical audience. Such a view was
held throughout the eighteenth century; Colman wrote that "it
must however be lamented that the Modern Tragick Stile, free, in-

deed, from the mad Flights of Dryden, and his Contemporaries, yet departs equally from Nature. . . . *Southerne* was the last of our Dramatick Writers, who was, in any Degree, possesst of that magnificent Plainness, which is the genuine Dress of Nature."[9] Francis Gentleman wrote that "Southerne, as a tragic writer, made very powerful attacks upon the tender passions, and is remarkably free in his versification."[10] In *A Comparison between the Two Stages*, during an interchange concerning *Oroonoko*, Southerne's language is praised:

R(amble). I have a particular regard for Mr. *Southern*'s Stile and agreeable Manner; there's a Spirit of Conversation in every thing he writes.

S(ullen). I think very few exceed him in the Dialogue; his Gallantry is natural, and after the real manner of the Town; his acquaintance with the best Company entered him into the secrets of their Intrigues, and no Man knew better the Way and Disposition of Mankind. But yet I must say, his Diction is commonly the best part of him, especially in Comedy; but in Tragedy he has once in this, and in one other, Drawn the Passions very well.[11]

We should recall that Dryden himself had written of Congreve:

In him all Beauties of this Age we see;
Etherege his Courtship, *Southern*'s Purity;
The Satire, Wit, and Strength of Manly *Witcherly*.

As Kaufman points out, Dryden here "is recommending Southerne's language; its clarity, its exactness of word choice, its freedom from antiquated or new-coined words."[12] But Kaufman himself complains that the characters are not differentiated enough by their language because of this purity.

The emphasis on Southerne's language, however, seems to have been not its purity, but its reality and its grace. In part this is why Southerne's diction does not fare well with Kaufman or with Bonamy Dobree, who complained that the rhythm of Southerne's verse "is hardly to be distinguished from that of prose."[13] But this is the very reason who so much of his work is powerful, because it approximates the rhythms of real speech. Of course this reaches its greatest effectiveness in prose, particularly in the comic work. If one compares Wishwell in *The Maid's Last Prayer* with Lady Wishfort in Congreve's *The Way of The World*, one sees how important Southerne's dialogue is for the development of Congreve's. In tragedy it is not the mixture of thought with feeling—Dobree complains that Southerne is one of those who thinks "that poetry can be made out of the emotions alone" and thus "his verse is like an embroidered garment covering a flimsy frame."[14] But it is the emphasis on feeling, the experience of passion by suffering individuals rather than the flights of bombast so prevalent in heroic drama, which strains after poetic effect, or the philosophizing of tragic poets which produces the frigid verse of Addison's *Cato*, that sustains the popularity of Southerne's creations on the stage. No critic or commentator refers to the intellectual content of Southerne's plays, only their emotional power.

This emotional power has long been recognized as a significant factor in the shaping of eighteenth-century drama, not only in tragedy, but in comedy as well. Nettleton wrote that Southerne's "most successful achievement was in the tragedies, which, at the close of the seventeenth century, help to bridge the gap between the Restoration and the Augustan Age. With some of Otway's dramatic pathos, though without his genius, Southerne points the way, perhaps, toward the sentimental drama of the eighteenth century. The school which Richard Steele is usually held to have founded seemed foreshadowed, however unconsciously, in the almost feminine appeal of Otway and Southerne to the sentiment of pity."[15] Nicoll concurs. "The fact that Southerne was one of the few dramatists whose work extends over the border of the two centuries and the fact that he mingled in such an artistic way the various elements heroic, Shakespearean, and pathetic make him one of the most interesting figures of the tragedy of the time. He stands with Rowe as one of the chief influences on the development of the later theatre."[16] Such a view lies behind Dodd's insistence that "his chief contribution to later drama was rather in the tone of pathetic sentiment which he helped to popularize and of which he was a chief continuator. Historically then, Southerne stands as the strongest link between Restoration and eighteenth century tragedy . . . and thus prepared the way for the final triumph in comedy of the Sentimental Muse."[17]

There can be little doubt about the connection among Otway, Southerne, and Rowe. We have seen the closeness between *The Orphan* and *The Fatal Marriage* and the echoes of *The Wives Excuse* in *The Fair Penitent;* the distressed heroine is equally a feature of the plays of Otway, Banks, Southerne, and Rowe. Hazlitt's linking of Southerne, Moore, and Lillo is suggestive of this same point.

Yet we should also note that very little specifically refers back to Southerne. The direct links to Southerne are usually weak efforts: George Powell's *Fatal Discovery* (1698) imitates the elements of domesticity and parallel tragic and comic plots to a rather tasteless degree;[18] a much later imitation of *The Fatal Marriage*, Osburne Sidney Wandesford's *Fatal Love, or, The Degenerate Brother* (1730) adds a good deal more bloody melodrama to a rather close rendering of Southerne's play, including a moral addressed to overstern parents. William Walker's *Victorious Love* (1698) is a rehash of the heroic elements of *Oroonoko*. None of these is successful commercially or artistically; nor are the plays most often acknowledged as indebted to Southerne's aid, Norton's *Pausanias*, Dennis's *Liberty Asserted*, Fenton's *Mariamne*, Hughes's *The Siege of Damascus*, and Madden's *Themistocles*. Southerne's direct influence in tragedy does not necessarily produce plays like his own and his indirect influence does not produce good ones. Thus in tragedy, at least, the influence of Southerne is primarily general and diffuse, although the early and continuous identification of him with Otway must surely suggest a continuing spirit that he provided the age.

In comedy, however, we are on somewhat firmer ground. Southerne assisted in the preparation of *The Old Bachelor*, Congreve's initial success, and in Cibber's *Love's Last Shift*. Moreover, as Harold Love has pointed out, the embodiment of comic ideals in the work of Congreve by Dryden first passed through the unsuccessful work of Southerne, particularly as evidenced by Dryden's epistle to *The Wives Excuse* and the commendatory verses to *The Double Dealer*.[19] Scouten suggests that "his work had little effect on the direction taken by the drama in the 1690's except for his noteworthy innovation of choosing a married couple to be the leading characters in a comedy, a striking deviation from the customary formula."[20] But it may be that just as the plight of Isabella and her domestic circumstances have an effect on the drama which follows, the adaptation by other playwrights of the married couple often subsumes into it some part of the unique vision Southerne used them to display, particularly in Crowne's *The Married Beau*, Vanbrugh's *The Provoked Wife*, and even Congreve's *The Double Dealer* and *The Way of The World*. These are not plays which simply use the married couple; they are plays which, as none but Southerne's before and only Farquhar's *The Beaux' Stratagem* until Ibsen, investigate the social and psychological significance of marriage in the current age. Thus we can agree with Scouten's judgment that "his acute psychological perception and his coldly realistic analyses of social and marital relationships make him one of the most artistic dramatists of the seventeenth century," but we should go on to see that his influence underlies the complex and profound insights of the best comedies of the decade. In another sense as well, his emphasis on the married couple, even when adapted by those who, like Cibber, do not share his view of marriage, leads to a proliferation of such emphases, until the Restoration conventions upon which they are founded are used up and discarded.

In sum, whether for his own accomplishments as an artist, a dramatist, a surveyor of the human condition, or for his position in a pivotal moment on the history of English drama, Thomas Southerne deserves our attention. No really complete understanding of Restoration drama, particularly in the 1690s, can be complete without reading his work, and it can only be hoped that he will soon receive his due. This work is but a step forward to that achievement.

Notes and References

For textual references I have used the 1721 edition of *The Works*, except for *Oroonoko*, where the 1976 edition was used, and *Money The Mistress*, from the 1774 edition of the *Works*.

Chapter One

1. *The Works of Alexander Pope* (London: J. & P. Knapton, 1751), VI, 82. See also Autrey Nell Wiley, ed., *Rare Prologues and Epilogues* (London: Allen and Unwin, 1940), pp. 67 - 72. The story appears in similar form everywhere it is recorded; only the amount varies. Supposedly the original source of the story is Southerne himself, who told it to Pope and Warburton. Warburton thought Dryden had raised the price from four to six guineas; Thomas Evans, the editor of *Plays Written by Thomas Southerne, Esq.* (London: T. Evans, 1774), thought the rise from five to ten (pp. 4 - 5). Evans also tells us of another occasion when Dryden asked Southerne how much he had made by one of his plays and Southerne, to Dryden's astonishment, confessed that he had cleared £700.

2. Charles Dalton, ed., *English Army Lists and Commission Registers, 1661 - 1714* (London: F. Edwards, 1892 - 1904), II, 29, 138. See also John Wendell Dodds, *Thomas Southerne, Dramatist* (New Haven: Yale Univ. Press, 1933), p. 5., n. 20.

3. Hugh MacDonald, *John Dryden. A Bibliography of Early Editions and Drydenia* (Oxford: Clarendon Press, 1939), p. 54.

4. *The Letters of John Dryden*, ed. Charles E. Ward (1942; reprinted N.Y.: AMS Press, 1965), p. 60.

5. Dryden, *Letters*, p. 54.

6. Charles Hopkins, *Epistolary Poems* (London: R. E. for J. Tonson, 1694), p. 7.

7. Hopkins, p. 10.

8. Colley Cibber, *An Apology for the Life of Colley Cibber*, ed. Robert W. Lowe (London: J. C. Nimmo, 1889), I, 212 - 13.

9. *The Critical Works of John Dennis*, ed. Edward Niles Hooker (Baltimore: Johns Hopkins Univ. Press, 1939), I, 324. *Letters by Several Eminent Persons Deceased*, ed. John Duncombe, 2nd. Ed. (London: J. Johnson, 1773), I, 251. Earl Harlan, *Elijah Fenton, 1683 - 1730* (Ph.D. diss., Univ. of Pennsylvania, 1937), p. 107.

10. *The Works of Alexander Pope*, ed. John Wilson Croker (London: J. Murray, 1872), VIII, 154.

11. Robert J. Jordan, "Thomas Southerne's Marriage," *Notes & Queries* N.S. 21 (August 1974): 293.

12. The other two successful playwrights of the 1690s continued in the theater, but Vanbrugh wrote no more original plays, except the fragment *A Journey to London*, and Cibber's work varies greatly in mode and influence. In effect, the new century was a new beginning with Farquhar coming into his own and Steele and Centlivre beginning their careers.

13. Southerne's notes on the life of Congreve are transcribed from British Museum, Add. MS. 4221 by Edmund Gosse, *The Life of William Congreve* (New York: Scribner's, 1924), pp. 175 - 76.

14. "On the Poets and Actors in King Charles II's Reign," *Gentleman's Magazine* 15 (February 1745): 99. See also Clifford Leech, "Thomas Southerne and 'On the Poets and Actors in King Charles II's Reign,'" *Notes & Queries* O.S. 154 (June 1933): 401 - 403.

15. Robert Jordan, in "Thomas Southerne, Agent," *Notes & Queries* 26 (February 1979): 14 - 21, refutes Clifford Leech, who, in "The Political 'Disloyalty' of Thomas Southerne," *Modern Language Review* 28 (October 1933): 421 - 30, used the same references to link the poet to a figure who opposed the execution of Jemmy Boucher, a Jacobite, and named other figures with Jacobite sympathies.

16. *Gentleman's Magazine* 16 (July 1746): 378.

17. Notably A. H. Scouten, "Notes toward a History of Restoration Comedy," *Philological Quarterly* 45 (January 1966): 62 - 70; John Harrington Smith, *The Gay Couple in Restoration Comedy* (Cambridge, Mass.: Harvard Univ. Press, 1948); Kenneth Muir, *The Comedy of Manners* (London: Hutchinson, 1970), pp. 84 - 92; and Robert D. Hume, *The Development of English Drama in the Late Seventeenth Century* (Oxford: Clarendon Press, 1976).

18. Hume, *Development of English Drama*, pp. 380 - 96, 411 - 22.

19. Smith deals with this subject in *Gay Couple*, pp. 108 - 40, and in "Shadwell, the Ladies, and the Change in Comedy," *Modern Philology* 46 (1948): 22 - 33.

20. P. F. Vernon, "Marriage of Convenience and the Moral Code of Restoration Comedy," *Essays in Criticism* 12 (1962): 370 - 87.

21. This aspect of Restoration comedy is surveyed in Robert D. Hume, "Marital discord in English Comedy from Dryden to Fielding," *Modern Philology* 74 (1977): 248 - 72.

22. Smith, *Gay Couple*, p. 167.

23. Eric Rothstein, *Restoration Tragedy: Form and the Process of Change* (Madison: Univ. of Wisconsin Press, 1967), p. 55.

24. Ibid., p. 59.

25. *The Island Queens*, though printed in 1684, was not acted until 1704, under the title *The Albion Queens*. *The Innocent Usurper*, although apparently written in 1684, was not published until 1693 and not acted until the following year. Both were banned for political reasons.

26. Rothstein, p. 110. My discussion of Restoration tragedy here is strongly influenced by Rothstein's study.

27. Dryden continued to write, producing *Don Sebastian*, his most pathetic tragedy, and his influence was substantial but not pervasive. Shadwell wrote until his death in 1692 and his five plays helped set the tone for reforming comedy. D'Urfey and Crowne continued to write as well, but they were not influential figures.

28. In the dedication to *The Wives Excuse* Southerne complained of "some of my Criticks, who were Affronted at Mrs. Friendall," because of her virtue, and believed the audience had not understood the play, Congreve expressed concern over the same problem in the dedication to *The Double Dealer*, particularly that "another very wrong objection has been made by some, who have not taken leisure to distinguish the characters" (*Complete Plays*, ed. Herbert Davis [Chicago: University of Chicago Press, 1967], p. 120). Similarly Crowne said in his Epistle to the Reader accompanying *The Married Beau* that some ladies were offended by the seduction and reformation of the heroine: "Now I thought the meditations of the ladies wou'd have slipt over the sinful part and dwelt upon the penitential. On the contrary, the contemplations of many ladies dwell all upon the sinful part; there they keep a pudder and bustle, and I cannot get them out of that apartment" (*Dramatic Works*, 1967, IV, 239). All these instances demonstrate the difficulty of getting an audience to accept departures from convention.

29. Peter Motteux, *Gentleman's Journal* 1 (January 1692): 33.

30. See Paul and Miriam Mueschke, *A New View of Congreve's Way of the World*. University of Michigan Contributions in Modern Philology, No. 23 (Ann Arbor, 1958).

31. Scouten, p. 66.

32. Harold Love, "Dryden, D'Urfey, and the Standard of Comedy," *Studies in English Literature 1500 - 1900* 13(1973): 422 - 36.

33. Nicholas Rowe, *The Fair Penitent*, ed. Malcolm Goldstein, Regents Restoration Drama Series (Lincoln: University of Nebraska Press, 1969), p.

34. Compare with Mrs. Friendall's speech in Act V: "The unjust World . . . condemn us to a Slavery for life: And if by separation we get free, then all our Husband's faults are laid on us: This hard Condition of a Woman's Fate, I've often weigh'd, therefore resolv'd to bear."

Chapter Two

1. *The London Stage*, Pt. 1, edited by William Lennep (Carbondale: Southern Illinois Univ. Press, 1965), p. 306.

2. In this period Aphra Behn produced *The Roundheads or, The Good Old Cause* (1681) and *The City Heiress, or, Sir Timothy Treatall* (1682), the title character a hit at Shaftesbury, who was also a target in Otway's *Venice Preserved* (1682). Crowne's *City Politiques* (1683); D'Urfey's *Sir Barnaby*

Whigg (1681) and *The Royalist* (1682)—these and the others are fairly overt in their political satire although the best of them endure as sound plays in their own right, the politics often being tangential to the primary drama. The most overtly political tragedies are Dryden and Lee's *The Duke of Guise* (1682) and Lee's *Constantine the Great* (1683), both Tory plays, and Settle's *Pope Joan, or, The Female Prelate* (1680), a Whig play.

3. The French novel was entitled *Tachmas, Prince de Perse, Nouvelle historique*, and dated 1676 also. Curiously P. Hamelius, in his edition of the play, *Thomas Southern's Loyal Brother: A Play on the Popish Plot* (Liège: H. Vaillant-Carmanne, 1911), mentions the English translation but makes no attempt to treat it as source material. Hamelius believed that the French novel was itself a *roman à clef* and that its rapid translation into English was due to its obvious parallels to the situation of the Stuart family in England (pp. 14 - 15).

4. Dodds, p. 35.

5. The term "serious plays" appears in Dryden's "Of Heroic Plays: An Essay" (1672). Geoffrey Marshall writes, "I have borrowed the term *serious* to indicate that I wish to consider a variety of plays having in common the fact that laughter and amusement are not their primary aims. The plays under study are sometimes tragedies and sometimes historical plays, tragicomedies, or other hybrid genres. I hope that the term *serious* will serve to circumvent questions of definition of genre" (*Restoration Serious Drama* [Norman: Univ. of Oklahoma Press, 1975], p. vii). Note that four of the plays collected by Bonamy Dobree in *Five Heroic Plays* (London: Oxford Univ. Press, 1960) are called tragedies on their original title pages, as is the archetypal heroic play, *The Conquest of Granada*.

6. In his introduction Hamelius draws a great many parallels between the French novel, the play, and the English political situation (pp. 14 - 19). In his scheme Seliman is Charles; Tachmas, James; Ismael (Allagolikan in the novel), the Earl of Shaftesbury; Begona, the widowed Queen Mother, Henrietta Maria, widow of Charles I, and mother of Charles and James. These parallels are so obvious and so inherent in the basic structure of the fictional and actual situations as to demand no comment. But then Hamelius begins to strain the parallels. He sees Semanthe as the Tory party, especially its women, particularly Queen Catherine, Charles's wife, but not Mary of Modena, wife of James, the Tachmas figure (p. 17). Sunamire and Arbanes, the conspiratorial siblings, Hamelius identifies as Lady Gerard of Bromley and a pastiche of her brother, Charles, Baron of Brandon; her nephew, Charles; and the Duke of Monmouth, Charles II's illegitimate son. The more specific Hamelius becomes the less credible his parallels seem and indeed his analysis of the political references in the play suffers from overingeniousness. Why is a reference to Seliman's birthday a reference to Charles's? Or Seliman's banquet in honor of Tachmas a parallel to the Lord Mayor's banquet in honor of Charles and James? The *roman à clef* dissolves into either vague allegory or parallels which can be found between any fictional character and any actual person.

7. Rothstein, p. 109.

8. Compare the scene in Act III of *All For Love* (III, 357 - 64), in John Dryden, *Four Tragedies*, ed. L. A. Beaurline and Fredson Bowers (Chicago: University of Chicago Press, 1967), p. 244.

9. The situation between Othello and Iago is echoed in several Restoration plays, particularly *The Villain* (1663), by Thomas Porter, centered on Malignii, and Henry Nevil Payne's *The Fatal Jealousy* (1672), where Jasper works on Antonio as Iago on Othello. In heroic drama, Otway's *Don Carlos* (1676) includes a scene in which Rui-Gomez maddens the jealous King Philip and drives him to consummate his marriage to a young wife by rape.

10. Thomas B. Stroup, "Philosophy and Drama," *London Times Literary Supplement*, January 19, 1933, p. 40. Stroup is speaking of evidence that Descartes was read by Restoration dramatists.

11. Dodds, p. 33.

12. John Harold Wilson, *A Preface to Restoration Drama* (Boston: Houghton Mifflin, 1965), p. 81.

13. Dodds, p. 47.

14. G. Wilson Knight, *The Golden Labyrinth* (London: Phoenix House, 1962), p. 168.

15. Montague Summers, *The Playhouse of Pepys* (New York: Macmillan, 1935), p. 67.

16. The curious impertinent motif occurs in various forms in the seventeenth-century drama, not all of them derived from Cervantes. A good discussion of the early material is A. S. W. Rosenbach, "The Curious-Impertinent in English Dramatic Literature before Shelton's Translation of *Don Quixote*," *Modern Language Notes* 17(1903): 357 - 67. In the Restoration the significant examples, in addition to *The Disappointment*, are Behn's *The Amorous Prince, or, The Curious Husband* (1671), which uses look-alike heroines to confuse matters and produce Fletcherian tragicomedy, and Crowne's *The Married Beau, or, The Curious Impertinent* (1694), as much indebted to Southerne's *The Wives Excuse* as the tradition, examining the triangle from the perspective of a satiric analysis of each member's motives.

17. *Othello*'s influence is found in other plays on the tragic consequences of jealousy: Sir Aston Cokain's *The Tragedy of Ovid* (1662) is principally about the tragic hastiness of Bassanes's action when he finds his wife alone with another man; Payne's *The Fatal Jealousy* is a bloody tragedy offering a baroque embellishment of Shakespeare's play.

18. This element appears in Dekker, Houghton, and Chettle's *Patient Grissil* (1599), Webster and Dekker's *Westward Ho* (1604), Wilkin's *Miseries of Enforced Marriage* (1607), and the anonymous *The Honest Lawyer* (1615); virtuous wives figure in several plays by Brome and Shirley and in D'Urfey's *The Virtuous Wife, or, Good Luck at Last* (1679).

19. The switch of partners in bed usually occurs in moralistic drama. Shakespeare used it twice, in *All's Well That Ends Well* (1602), where the wife replaces the young virgin, and in *Measure for Measure* (1604), where

Mariana, Angelo's mistress, replaces the chaste Isabella. Massinger used it in *The Parliament of Love* (1624) and Brome in *The English Moor, or, The Mock Marriage* (1637), where a rake's mistress takes the place of the virtuous wife, and in *A Mad Couple Well Match't* (1636). Shirley used a variation in *The Gamester* (1633). In the Restoration deliberate substitution to avoid adultery is rare, occurring principally here and in Cibber's *Love's Last Shift* (1695), where the wife seduces the husband while he believes she is merely a wanton. In all of these cases, the wastrel who enjoys the woman has a change of heart.

20. Dodds, p. 48.

Chapter Three

1. Judith Milhous and Robert D. Hume, "Dating Play Premieres from Publication Data, 1660 - 1700," *Harvard Library Bulletin* 22(1974): 398.

2. Robert J. Jordan, "Mrs. Behn and *Sir Anthony Love*," *Restoration and Eighteenth Century Theatre Research* 12(1973): 58 - 59.

3. As in Verole's "Fall on, and kill the Ravisher—Come, my fair Fugitive, you must along with me," and in Charlott's explanation of her disguise, both Act V of the play and pp. 345 and 346, respectively, of *The Novels of Aphra Behn*, ed. Ernest A. Baker (1913; reprinted Westport Conn.: Greenwood Press, 1969).

4. Heywood's *The Fair Maid of the West* (1607) and Middleton and Dekker's *The Roaring Girl, or, Moll Cutpurse* (1611) both center on women in male dress. Restoration prototypes for Sir Anthony include the characters in the anonymous *The Woman Turn'd Bully* (1675), where "Sir Thomas Whimsey" is as much a swaggerer as Sir Anthony, and Shadwell's *The Woman Captain* (1679), a straight farce about a wife's revenge on her husband.

5. Hume, *Development of English Drama*, p. 385.

6. Behn's Charlott is more rational and sympathetic: after an extended explanation she says, "And for my part, Sir, I was not so much in love with Rinaldo, as I was out of love with the nunnery; and took any opportunity to quit a life so absolutely contrary to my humour." Behn adds, "She spoke this with a gaiety so brisk, and an air so agreeable that Vernole found it touched his heart" (Behn, p. 346).

7. Dodds, p. 73.

8. Allardyce Nicoll, *A History of English Drama 1660 - 1900* (Cambridge, Eng.: Cambridge Univ. Press, 1952), I, 240.

9. Ben Ross Schneider, Jr., *The Ethos of Restoration Comedy* (Urbana: Univ. of Illinois Press, 1971), p. 112.

10. Knight, pp. 138 - 40.

11. Dodds, p. 67.

12. Summers, *Playhouse of Pepys*, p. 243. Few such lampoons are generally available, but reference to them is also made in *Poems on Affairs*

of State, Volume 5: 1688 - 1697, ed. William J. Cameron (New Haven: Yale Univ. Press, 1971), p. 38.

13. Muir, p. 85.

14. Dodds, p. 65.

15. Ibid., p. 67.

16. Montague Summers, "The Source of Southerne's *The Fatal Marriage," Modern Language Review* 11(1916): 155.

17. Muir, p. 86.

18. Hume, *Development of English Drama,* p. 386.

19. Nicoll, p. 240.

Chapter Four

1. *The Wives Excuse, or, Cuckolds Make Themselves,* ed. Ralph R. Thornton (Wynnewood, Pa.: Livingston Pub. Co., 1973), p. 15.

2. See particularly Shadwell's *Epsom Wells* (1672), Otway's *Friendship in Fashion* (1678), and Behn's *Sir Patient Fancy* (1678) and *The Lucky Chance* (1686).

3. James E. Sutherland, *English Literature in the Later Seventeenth Century* (Oxford: Oxford Univ. Press, 1969), p. 145.

4. Nicoll claimed "its main point of interest for us is an historical one—the introduction in the comedy itself of a reference to Southerne's own work, a sort of premonition of Shavian methods of self-advertisement" (pp. 240 - 41). It would be more accurate to consider the treatment of the play here with Molière's defense of his own work in *La Critique de l'École des femmes* and *Impromptu de Versailles* (both 1663) and Wycherley's adaptation of Molière's techniques in the discussion of *The Country Wife* inserted in *The Plain Dealer.* In none of these, however, is the discussion of the playwright's work about the play the audience is at that moment attending.

5. Smith, *Gay Couple,* p. 146.

6. Muir, p. 91.

7. Smith, *Gay Couple,* p. 148.

8. Hume, *Development of English Drama,* p. 387.

9. Sutherland, p. 145.

10. Thornton, p. 38. The quotation is from Cicero.

11. See Congreve's preface to *The Double Dealer* and Crowne's to *The Married Beau* for further evidence of the gap between expectation and execution.

12. Nicoll, p. 240.

13. Dodds, p. 80.

14. Anthony Kaufman, " 'This Hard Condition of a Woman's Fate': Southerne's *The Wives Excuse," Modern Language Quarterly* 34: 1(1973): 44.

15. *Gentleman's Journal* 1(1692): 33.

16. Smith, *Gay Couple*, p. 144.
17. Ibid., p. 188.
18. Hume, *Development of English Drama*, pp. 386 - 87.
19. Scouten, p. 66.
20. I have explored this group of plays at length in "The Problematics of Marriage: English Comedy 1688 - 1710" (Ph.D. diss., Univ. of Iowa, 1975).

Chapter Five

1. Muir, p. 94.
2. Hume, *Development of English Drama*, p. 388.
3. Smith, *Gay Couple*, p. 144.
4. Nicoll notes that "the situation appears with variations in *The Mall* (D.L. 1674)," suggesting that Lady Malepert's discovery that she spent the night with Gayman, not Sir Ruff (Nicoll calls him Valentine by mistake), is comparable to Mrs. Wouldbee sleeping with Courtall, thinking him her husband, Lovechange (p. 241). (Dodds, citing Nicoll, calls him Lovemore.) But Courtall is as mistaken as the wife; and the husband has arranged the assignation, unlike Gayman's substitution of himself. A closer similarity is with Aphra Behn's *The Lucky Chance*, where a gallant also named Gayman wins a night with Lady Fulbank at cards. His love for her excuses him to her; her husband's avarice in prostituting her while gambling separates them. The nearest analogue to Lady Malepert's change of feeling—albeit mistaken—is Beatrice Joanna's change of feeling from loathing to doting upon DeFlores in Middleton's *The Changeling* (1622).
5. Dodds, p. 92.
6. Nicoll, p. 241.
7. *Gentleman's Journal* 2(1693): 28.
8. Hume, *Development of English Drama*, p. 388.
9. Nor could Congreve, Crowne, and Vanbrugh. The tension between what Hume calls "hard" and "humane" comedy vibrates through all their original work of the decade.
10. The quotation is from Horace, *Epistoles*, Book 2, Epistle 1. The translation here is from Horace, *Satires, Epistles, and Ars Poetica*, tr. H. Ruston Fairclough, revised, Loeb Classical Library (Cambridge: Harvard University Press, 1947).

Chapter Six

1. John Downes, *Roscius Anglicanus*, ed. Montague Summers (1929; reprinted New York: B. Blom, 1968), p. 38.
2. Quoted in the *London Stage*, Pt. 1, p. 432.
3. Ibid., p. 434.
4. *Isabella, or, The Fatal Marriage* (London: J. Hoey, P. Wilson, W. Slator, 1758). The advertisement to the play was written by Garrick. See

Letters of David Garrick, ed. David M. Little and George M. Kahrl (Cambridge, Mass.: Belknap Press, 1963); I, 271; II, 764.

5. A striking portrait of Mrs. Siddons as Isabella and her son Henry as Isabella's son can be found in *The Revels History of English Drama,* VI (London: Methuen, 1976), plate 34, between p. 226 - 27.

6. Dodds, pp. 126 - 27.

7. See George C. D. Odell, *Annals of the New York Stage* (New York: Columbia Univ. Press, 1927 - 31), V. I - V; Nelle Smither, *A History of the English Theatre in New Orleans* (1944; reprinted New York: B. Blom, 1967), p. 344; Reese D. James, *Old Drury of Philadelphia* (1932; reprinted New York: Johnson Reprint, 1968), pp. 643, 660, 678; and George O. Seilhamer, *History of the American Theatre* (1888 - 91; reprinted New York: B. Blom, 1968), V. II, III. Odell includes a portrait of Mary Barnes as Isabella in Volume II, opposite p. 270.

8. Frederick M. Link, *Aphra Behn,* Twayne's English Authors Series (New York, 1968), p. 144.

9. The tragic plot directly inspired one outright imitation, Osburne Sidney Wandesford's *Fatal Love, or, The Degenerate Brother* (1730), which adds a little more bloodshed but concludes: "Parents take warning by these Mighty Ills,/Force not your Children's Hands against their wills. . . . For Shame and Horror ever will attend/Base and unworthy actions in the End."

10. *The Humours of Purgatory* (1716), a funny, lively farce by Benjamin Griffin, is sometimes associated with the comic plot of *The Fatal Marriage;* but its connection is tenuous, existing only in the wife's name, Julia, and the husband's going to Purgatory. Here he is Don Lopez di Porto Vitranto, a hypochrondriac. The subjects of Southerne's plot are never raised.

11. *Isabella,* p. 3.

12. David Erskine Baker et al., *Biographia Dramatica; or, A Companion to the Playhouse* (1812; reprinted New York: AMS Press, 1966), II, 230.

13. Richard Cumberland, *The British Drama* (London: C. Cooke, 1817), XIV, x - xi.

14. John Genest, *Some Account of the English Stage from the Restoration in 1660 - 1832* (Bath: H. E. Carrington, 1832), II, 56 - 57.

15. Dodds appends a list of editions of *The Fatal Marriage* and *Oroonoko,* pp. 220 - 25. The fame of *The Fatal Marriage* was international as well, having been translated into French in 1749 and into German in 1788 and after.

16. Dodds, p. 113.

17. Nicoll, p. 154.

18. John Loftis, Richard Southern, Marion Jones, and A. H. Scouten, *The Revels History of Drama in English,* Volume V: 1660 - 1750 (London: Methuen, 1976), p. 279.

19. Hume, *Development of English Drama,* p. 403.

20. Ibid., pp. 402 - 403.

Chapter Seven

1. Cibber, *Apology*, II, 311. Halifax, of course, had no power to order such a change of casting, but he may have influenced Verbruggen's selection.

2. Garrick, *Letters*, I, 316 - 19; II, 764.

3. William Hazlitt, *The Complete Works*, ed. P. P. Howe (London: J. M. Dent, 1933), VI, 359. His review of Kean's performance appeared in the *Examiner* for January 26, 1817 (XVIII, 215 - 18).

4. Thomas Southerne, *Oroonoko*, ed. Maximillian E. Novak and David Stuart Rodes, Regents Restoration Drams (Lincoln: Univ. of Nebraska Press, 1976). p. xvi. They note that *Oroonoko* had 315 performances in the eighteenth century, compared to *The Fatal Marriage*'s 188, and that it was "particularly popular as a play for visiting dignitaries, for benefit performances, and for introducing young new actors to the London theater."

5. Dodds, pp. 223 - 25. *The Fatal Marriage* had fifty-three printings.

6. Because of its subject matter, *Oroonoko* was not played in Liverpool, the heart of the English slave trade, nor, one suspects, in new Orleans, where *Isabella* had been so successful for several actresses. In addition to Ferriar's adaptation, we should also mention a burletta, *Oroonoko, The Royal Slave*, performed in 1813, and Thomas Merton's *The Slave*, a combination of *Oroonoko* and a German melodrama, *Pizarro*, into a musical form. William Charles MacReady played Gambia in this short-lived play November 12, 1816.

7. Thomas Southerne, *Oroonoko*, The Black Heritage Library Collection (Freeport, New York: Books for Libraries, 1969). The facsimile is taken from the copy of the 1739 edition in the Fisk University Library Negro Collection, which the title page calls "the 4th edition Correcteed." As Dodds points out, this editon was printed in Dublin and follows exactly the 1721 edition of the *Works*. The facsimile is reprinted without introduction or critical apparatus.

8. *The Works of Aphra Behn*, ed. Montague Summers (London: W. Heinemann, 1915), VI, 127.

9. However, Lucy Welldon is one of the characters and *The Widow Ranter* is dedicated to Lucy Weldon, wife of Sir George Weldon. William R. Richardson claims Wycherley's *The Plain Dealer* and the anonymous *Counterfeit Bridegroom* as sources, but on shaky grounds ("The Life and Works of Thomas Southerne," Ph.D. diss., Harvard, 1933). As Dodds points out, "the situation is an old one, used by Southerne before in *Sir Anthony Love*, in which a young woman disguised as a man woos and marries another woman, putting to bed with her a friend of whose manhood there is no question" (p. 148).

10. G. Blakemore Evans, ed., *The Plays and Poems of William Cartwright* (Madison: Univ. of Wisconsin Press, 1951), suggests that Southerne modeled III, ii on Cartwright's II, vi of *The Royal Slave* (1625) and asks, "Is it perhaps significant that Southerne dropped the subtitle of

the novel?" (597). The answer is "No," since a reading of the two scenes finds that the circumstances and the modes of argument are entirely different.

11. See especially Hoxie Neal Fairchild, *The Noble Savage, A Study in Romantic Naturalism* (New York: Russell & Russell, 1928) and Wylie Sypher, *Guinea's Captive Kings: British Anti-Slavery Literature of the XVIIIth Century* (Chapel Hill, N.C.: Univ. North Carolina Press, 1942).

12. All quotations are from the Novak/Rodes edition.

13. *The Monthly Review, or, Literary Journal* 78(1788): 522.

14. *A Comparison between the Two Stages: A Late Restoration Book of the Theatre*, ed. Staring B. Wells (Princeton, N.J.: Princeton Univ. Press, 1942), pp. 20 - 21.

15. *A Comparison*, p. 19.

16. *Oroonoko*, ed. John Hawkesworth (London, 1759), quoted in *The Critical Review, or, Annals of Literature* 8(1759): 480.

17. Anne Marie MacKenzie, *Slavery, or, The Times* (Dublin: P. Wogan, P. Byrne, J. Moore, 1793), p. 121.

18. Hannah More, "The Slave Trade," *The Works of Hannah More* (Cork: T. White, 1789), p. 27.

19. Hawkesworth, quoted in *Critical Review*, p. 480.

20. Hawkesworth, p. 481.

21. *Critical Review*, p. 480. Dodds ascribes the review to Samuel Johnson (152, n. 61).

22. John Ferriar, *The Prince of Angola* (Manchester: J. Harrop, 1788), p. 1.

23. Baker, III, 103.

24. Cumberland, XI, iv.

25. William Archer, *The Old Drama and the New, An Essay in Revaluation* (Boston: Small, Maynard & Co., 1903), p. 169.

26. Genest, II, 71.

27. Rothstein, p. 146.

28. Hume, *Development of English Drama*, pp. 425 - 26. A further discussion of this topic is Michael M. Cohen, " 'Mirth and Grief Together': Plot Unity in Southerne's *Oroonoko*," *Xavier University Studies* 11:3(1972): 13 - 17.

29. Nicoll, p. 155.

30. Quoted in Novak/Rodes, pp. xvii - xviii.

Chapter Eight

1. In a letter dated April 11, 1700, Dryden writes, "Southerne's tragedy, calld the Revolt of Capuoa, will be playd at Betterton's House within this Fortnight. I am out with that Company & therefore if I can help it, will not read it before 'tis Acted; though the author much desires I shou'd" (*Letters*, p. 136).

2. Downes, p. 45.

3. It is difficult to know how significant Southerne's contribution was. As Gary T. Anderberg points out, "since Dryden, who was always quick to acknowledge his indebtedness to friends, does not mention Southerne in either the Preface or the Dedication, one may assume that his contribution was of minor importance to the essential design and temper of the play" ("*Cleomenes* and Affective Tragedy," *Essays in Literature* 3[1976]: 51).

4. Hume, *Development of English Drama*, pp. 400 - 440, 453 - 55.

5. *Livy*, translated by Frank Gardner Moore, revised, Loeb Classical Library (Cambridge, Mass.: Harvard Univ. Press, 1951), XIV, 7.

6. *Livy*, XIV, 13 - 17; Southerne, pp. 274 - 92.

7. Pacuvius's son is not named in Livy, and his name seems to stem from the misprint, "Calavius filius perholla" for "Calavius filius perlici ad" (*Livy*, XIV, 24). Perolla is the son in Roger Boyle, Earl of Orrery's romance, *Parthenissa* (1676), and there is reference there to this incident, but Southerne shows no evidence of its influence and indeed Boyle hurries on to Perolla's heroics and melodramatic love for Izadora, niece of Magius. The story in Boyle ends happily; it serves as the basis for Cibber's *Perolla and Izadora* (1706).

8. *Livy*, XIV, 23 - 29.

9. *Livy*, VII, 47 - 55.

10. Dodds, p. 168.

11. A. W. Ward, *A History of English Dramatic Literature to the Death of Queen Anne*, 2nd. ed. (1899; reprinted New York: Ungar, 1970), III, 423.

12. Hume, *Development of English Drama*, p. 455.

13. *Works of Mr. Thomas Southerne* (London: J. Tonson, 1713), I, preface.

14. The epistle is reprinted at the head of all three editions of his works.

15. *Works of Mr. Thomas Southerne* (London: J. Tonson, 1721), p. 341.

16. *William Congreve: Letters & Documents*, ed. John C. Hodges (New York: Harcourt, Brace & World, 1964), p. 231.

17. *Works* (1721), p. 343.

18. Genest, III, 8.

19. *Calendar of the Manuscripts of the Marquis of Bath*, (Hereford, Eng.: Historical Manuscripts Commission 1908), III, 476 - 77. Prior refers to the play again in "The Turtle and the Sparrow," in the lines "And as Tom Southerne wisely says,/'No other fault had she in Life/But only that she was my Wife' " (ll. 221 - 23). His editors believe the reference is to *The Spartan Dame*, I, ii: "But she's my Wife—and nothing but a Wife, With all her Charms, cou'd stale so soon." See *The Literary Works of Matthew Prior*, ed. H. Bunker Wright and Monroe K. Spears (Oxford: Clarendon Press, 1959), I, 536; II, 987.

20. It was this play that led Pope to describe him as one "whom heav'n sent down to raise/The price of prologues and of plays" (*Minor Poems*, ed. Norman Ault [London: Methuen, 1964], p. 399). An epigram, "In Behalf of

Mr. Southerne to the Duke of Argyle," seems to have been inspired by Southerne's dedication of *The Spartan Dame* (*Minor Poems*, pp. 214 - 15).

21. The motto of the play, "Pellex ego factis sororis," is from Ovid's *Metamorphoses*, the story of the rape of Philomela by her sister's husband, Tereus. The more accurate transcription, "paelex ego facta sororis," is translated as "I have become a concubine, my sister's rival" in Ovid, *Metamorphoses*, translated by Frank Justus Miller, Loeb Classical Library (Cambridge: Harvard Univ. Press, 1925), pp. 324 - 25.

22. Genest, III, 7.

23. Dodds, p. 191.

24. *Works of Alexander Pope*, Volume VIII, ed. John Wilson Croker (London: J. Murray, 1872), p. 111.

25. Ibid., p. 112.

26. Benjamin Victor, *The History of the Theatres of London and Dublin* (London: T. Davies, 1761), II, 152.

27. Genest, III, 180.

28. Comtesse Marie d'Aulnoy, *The Ingenious and Diverting Letters of the Lady—Travels into Spain*, 4th ed. (London: Samuel Crouch, 1697), pp. 67 - 85. The character of the widow is introduced earlier, on p. 59.

29. Dodds, p. 202.

Chapter Nine

1. The fullest discussion is in Clifford Leech, "The Political Disloyalty of Thomas Southerne," *Modern Language Review* 28(1933): 421 - 30.

2. Dodds, p. 205.

3. Ibid., p. 207.

4. Ibid., p. 208.

5. Baker, I, 681.

6. John Sheffield, Duke of Buckinghamshire, in *Minor English Poets 1660 - 1780*, compiled by David P. French (New York: B. Blom, 1967), II, 654.

7. *The Grove, or, A Collection of Original Poems, Translations, etc.* (London: A. Baldwin, 1721), pp. 129, 140 - 41.

8. Hazlitt, V, 199; VI, 359.

9. "Critical Reflections on the Old English Writers," in *The Dramatick Works of Philip Massinger*, ed. Thomas Coxeter (London: T. Davies, 1761), I, 20.

10. *The Dramatic Censor, or, Critical Companion* (London: J. Bell, 1770), II, 470.

11. *A Comparison*, p. 19.

12. Kaufman, p. 37.

13. Bonamy Dobree, *Restoration Tragedy* (Oxford: Clarendon Press, 1929), p. 63.

14. Ibid., p. 64.

15. George Henry Nettleton, *English Drama of the Restoration and Eighteenth Century (1642 - 1780)* (1932; reprinted New York: Cooper Square Pub., 1968), p. 119.

16. Nicoll, p. 155.

17. Dodds, p. 217.

18. The play sets a cuckolding intrigue against a plot involving double incest which is as "innocent" as Isabella's adultery.

19. Love, pp. 422 - 36.

20. Scouten, *The Revels History*, V, 214.

Selected Bibliography

PRIMARY SOURCES

The Loyal Brother, or, The Persian Prince. London: Wm. Cademan, 1682.
The Disappointment, or, The Mother in Fashion. London: J. Hindmarsh, 1684.
Sir Anthony Love, or, The Rambling Lady. London: J. Fox, 1691.
The Wives Excuse, or, Cuckolds Makes Themselves. London: Samuel Brisco, 1692.
The Maid's Last Prayer, or, Any Rather Than Fail. London: R. Bentley, 1693.
The Fatal Marriage, or, The Innocent Adultery. London: J. Tonson, 1694.
Oroonoko. London: H. Playford, B. Tooke, S. Buckley, 1695.
The Fate of Capua. London: B. Tooke, 1700.
The Works of Mr. Thomas Southerne, 2 vols. London: J. Tonson, 1713. Contains the first eight plays in chronological order, a preface by Southerne, and Fenton's "Epistle to Mr. Southerne."
The Spartan Dame. London: W. Chetwood, 1719.
The Works of Mr. Thomas Southerne, 2 vols. London: J. Tonson, 1721. Deletes 1713 preface; adds *The Spartan Dame* with all the lines deleted from the first edition and additional remarks.
Money The Mistress. London: J. Tonson, 1726.
Plays Written by Thomas Southerne, Esq., 3 vols. London: T. Evans, 1774. All plays reset; Fenton's "Epistle" precedes *Spartan Dame;* adds "Account of the Life and Writings of the Author" by Thomas Evans and a letter by the Earl of Orrery.
Thomas Southerne's Loyal Brother: A Play on the Popish Plot. Ed. P. Hamelius. Bibliotheque de la Faculté de Philosophie et Lettres de L'Université de Liège, Fascicule XX. Liège: H. Vaillant-Carmanne, 1911.
The Wives Excuse, or, Cuckolds Make themselves. Ed. Ralph R. Thornton. Wynnewood, Pa.: Livington Publishing Company, 1973.
Oroonoko. Ed. Maximillian E. Novak and David Stuart Rodes. Regents Restoration Drama Series. Lincoln: University of Nebraska Press, 1976.

SECONDARY SOURCES

ALKOFER, DANIEL W. "A Note on the Staging of *Money The Mistress* in 1726," *Restoration and 18th Century Theatre Research* 11(May 1972):

31 - 32. Concerns possible significance of symbols in the promptbook of the play in the Bodleian library.

ALLEMAN, GELLERT SENCER. *Matrimonial Law and the Materials of Restoration Comedy*. Wallingford: Univ. of Pennsylvania Press, 1942. Thorough compilation of plays using one or more elements of contemporary marriage law.

AVERY, EMMETT L., et al. *The London Stage, 1660 - 1800*. 5 pts. in 11 vols. Carbondale: Southern Illinois Univ. Press, 1960 - 1968. Indispensable resource for theatrical information; parts I and II particularly detail information on performances of Southerne's plays.

BEHN, APHRA. *The Works of Aphra Behn*. Ed. Montague Summers. 5 vols. London, 1915; reprinted New York: Benjamin Blom, 1967. Volume 5 collects her prose narratives, among them Southerne's sources.

_____. *Oroonoko, or, The Royal Slave*. Introduction by Lore Metzger. New York: W. W. Norton & Company, 1973. Discusses the novel in connection with her drama.

BERNBAUM, ERNEST. *The Drama of Sensibility*. Boston: Ginn & Company, 1915. A sound introduction to sentimental comedy, though uneven concerning Southerne's influence.

BOWERS, FREDSON C. "The Supposed Cancel in Southerne's *The Disappointment* Reconsidered," *Library* 5th Series, V (1950): 140 - 49. Resolves an issue concerning the printing of the play.

CIBBER, COLLEY. *An Apology for the Life of Mr. Colley Cibber*. Ed. Robert Lowe. 2 vols. London: J. C. Nimmo, 1889. An important overview of the London stage during the 1690s and early eighteenth century.

COHEN, MICHAEL M. " 'Mirth and Grief Together': Plot Unity in Southerne's *Oroonoko*," *Xavier University Studies* 11(Winter 1972): 13 - 17. Discusses the relationship between the tragic and comic plots.

A Comparison between the Two Stages. Ed. Staring B. Wells. Princeton: Princeton Univ. Press, 1942. Contemporary survey of the stage providing a context for Southerne's work.

DENNIS, JOHN. *The Critical Works of John Dennis*. Ed. Edward Hooker. 2 vols. Baltimore: John Hopkins Univ. Press, 1938 - 43. Collected writing by a leading dramatic critic and theorist of the Dryden circle.

DODDS, JOHN WENDELL. *Thomas Southerne, Dramatist*. Yale Studies in English, LXXXI. New Haven: Yale Univ. Press, 1933. A thorough survey of material concerning Southerne, marred by moralistic outrage over the comedies and a rather single-minded view of his significance.

DRYDEN, JOHN. *The Critical and Miscellaneous Prose Works*. Ed. Edmund Malone. London: Cadell and Davies, 1800. V. I, Part I, 176 - 77. Reprints Southerne's 1737 letter to Rawlinson about his life.

_____. *The Letters of John Dryden*. Ed. Charles E. Ward. 1942; reprinted New York: AMS Press, Inc., 1965. Gives some indication of the relationship among Dryden, Southerne, and Congreve.

FINCH, G. J. "Hawkesworth's adaptation of Southerne's *Oroonoko*," *Restoration and 18th Century Theatre Research* 16 (May 1977): 40 - 43. Points out the shift from the psychology of slavery to the effects of it in Hawkesworth's revision.

GOSSE, EDMUND. *The Life of William Congreve.* New York: Charles Scribner's Sons, 1924. Includes in an appendix Southerne's notes to a life of Congreve.

HAMELIUS, PAUL. "The Source of Southerne's 'Fatal Marriage,' " *Modern Language Review* 4 (1909): 352 - 56. Ascribes Spanish sources for the play.

HUME, ROBERT D. *The Development of English Drama in the Late Seventeenth Century.* Oxford: Clarendon Press, 1976. A successful attempt to provide a theatrical background and context for the reading of Restoration drama.

_____. "Marital Discord in English Comedy from Dryden to Fielding," *Modern Philology* 74(February 1977): 248 - 72. Surveys the subject with special attention to 1690s and *The Wives Excuse*.

HUMMEL, RAY O., JR. "A Further Note on Southerne's *The Disappointment*," *Library* 5th Series, I (1946): 67 - 69. Responds to Leech's discussion of a cancel in the text.

JACOB, GILES, *The Poetical Register; or, The Lives and Characters of the English Dramatic Poets.* London, 1719; reprinted New York: Garland Publishing, Inc., 1970. Earliest Southerne biography and review of his work through *The Fate of Capua*.

JORDAN, ROBERT, J. "Mrs. Behn and *Sir Anthony Love*," *Restoration and 18th Century Theatre Research* 12(1973): 58 - 59. Argues that *The Lucky Mistake* is the main source of the play.

_____. "Thomas Southerne, Agent," *Notes & Queries* New Series XXVI (February 1979): 14 - 21. Looks at evidence for Southerne's employment during 1706 - 1714.

_____. "Thomas Southerne's Marriage," *Notes & Queries* New Series XXI (August 1974): 293 - 95. Analyzes current information about whom Southerne married and when.

KAUFMAN, ANTHONY. " 'This Hard Condition of a Woman's Fate': Southerne's *The Wives' Excuse*," *Modern Language Quarterly* 34(March 1973): 36 - 47. Focuses on Mrs. Friendall and her dilemma in the context of other comedies of marriage.

LANGHANS, EDWARD A. "Three Early Eighteenth-Century Manuscript Promptbooks," *Modern Philology* 65(November 1967): 114 - 29. Records the prompt notes for the staging of *Money the Mistress* and plays by Theobald and Settle.

LEECH, CLIFFORD M. "A Cancel in Southerne's *The Disappointment*," *Library* 4th Series, XIII (1933): 395 - 98. Initiates the series on this topic settled by Bowers.

———. "Congreve and the Century's End," *Philological Quarterly* 41(1962): 275 - 93. Generally sound analysis of the 1690s, particularly Congreve's part in them, and the melding of old and new traditions.

———. "Southerne's *The Disappointment*," *Library* 5th Series, II (June 1947): 64. A response to Hummel's article.

———. "The Political 'Disloyalty' of Thomas Southerne," *Modern Language Review* 28(1933): 421 - 30. Prints and discusses three letters he attributes to Southerne and reviews the political and literary context for attribution.

———. "Thomas Southerne," *Times Literary Supplement*, December 8, 1932, p. 243. Supplements Mallery's correction of the Southerne article in the *Dictionary of National Biography*.

———. "Thomas Southerne and 'On the Poets and Actors in King Charles II's Reign'," *Notes & Queries* Old Series, CLXIV (1933): 401 - 403. Argues for Southerne's authorship of a brief review of the Restoration theater.

LINK, FREDERICK M. *Aphra Behn*. Twayne's English Authors Series. New York: Twayne Publishers, Inc., 1968. Judicious survey of her works, including the novels which served as Southerne's sources.

LOFTIS, JOHN. *Comedy and Society from Congreve to Fielding*. Stanford Studies in Language and Literature, No. 19. Stanford: Stanford Univ. Press, 1958. Useful discussion of the social background of the 1690s and early eighteenth century.

LOFTIS, JOHN, et al. *The Revels History of Drama in English*. Volume 5: 1660 - 1750. London: Methuen & Co., Ltd., 1976. Helpful survey, with sound comments on Southerne's work.

LOVE, HAROLD. "Dryden, D'Urfey, and the Standard of Comedy," *Studies in English Literature 1500 - 1900* 13(Summer 1973): 422 - 36. Includes a discussion of Southerne's role in a controversy over the purpose of comedy altering Dryden's stance.

———. "The Printing of *The Wives Excuse* (1692)," *Library* 5th Series, XXV (1970): 344 - 49. Responds to Sweney about the printing of the quarto with Dryden's dedication.

———. "The States of Southerne's *The Spartan Dame*, 1719," *Library* 5th Series, XXXI (1976): 369 - 76. Examines variants in first three "editions" printed in 1719.

———. "The Texts of Southerne's *The Spartan Dame*," *Bulletin of the Bibliographical Society of Australia and New Zealand* 3 (October 1971): 54 - 59. Lists stages of evolution for the play up until the 1721 edition and speculates on the relation of the 1719 edition to the final edition.

MALLERY, R. D. "Thomas Southerne," *Times Literary Supplement*, December 1, 1932, p. 923. Corrects Ward's article in the *DNB*.

McDONALD, MARGARET LAMB. *The Independent Woman in Restoration Comedy of Manners*. Salzburg Studies in English Literature: Poetic

Drama and Poetic Theory. Institut für Englische Sprache and Literatur. Salzburg: Univ. Salzburg, 1976. Discussion of the female characters of several playwrights, including Southerne, in their changing social context.

MILHOUS, JUDITH, and HUME, ROBERT D., "Dating Play Premieres from Publication Data, 1660 - 1700," *Harvard Library Bulletin* 22(1974): 374 - 405. A corrective to the dating of play performances previously conjectured, including some by Southerne.

MISH, CHARLES C., ed. *Restoration Prose Fiction 1660 - 1700*. Lincoln: Univ. of Nebraska Press, 1970. Representative anthology, including Behn's *History of the Nun*, source for *The Fatal Marriage*.

MOTTEUX, PETER. *The Gentleman's Journal, or, The Monthly Miscellany*. 3 vols. London, 1691 - 1694. Reprints songs from the plays and comments on Southerne and his contemporaries.

MUIR, KENNETH. *The Comedy of Manners*. London: Hutchinson Univ. Library, 1970. A sound and important analysis of Southerne's comedies.

NICOLL, ALLARDYCE. *A History of English Drama 1600 - 1900*. 6 vols. Cambridge: Cambridge Univ. Press, 1959. The first two volumes cover the Restoration and early eighteenth century; still a valuable study of the theater.

NORTON, RICHARD. *Pausanias, The Betrayer of His Country*. London: A. Roper, E. Wilinson, R. Clavell, 1696. The preface is by Southerne.

NOVAK, MAXIMILLIAN E. *William Congreve*. Twayne's English Authors Series. New York: Twayne Publishers, Inc., 1971. Particularly good introductory chapter on the milieu of the 1690s.

"On the Poets and Actors in King Charles II's Reign," *Gentleman's Magazine* 15(1745): 99. Attributed to Southerne by Leech.

ORRERY PAPERS. Ed. The Countess of Cork and Orrery. 2 vols. London: Duckworth & Company, 1903. Includes in Vol. I a large number of letters to and about Southerne by John Boyle, Earl of Orrery.

RICHARDSON, WILLIAM RITTENHOUSE. "The Life and Works of Thomas Southerne," Ph.D., diss., Harvard University, 1933. Attention is chiefly to sources and influences, much of it overimaginative or unreliable.

ROTHSTEIN, ERIC. *Restoration Tragedy: Form and the Process of Change*. Madison: Univ. of Wisconsin Press, 1967. The best modern study of Restoration tragedy and an important source for the background of Southerne's serious drama.

SCOUTEN, A. H. "Notes toward a History of Restoration Comedy," *Philological Quarterly* 45(January 1966): 62 - 70. Important article recognizing the existence of a "marriage group" of plays initiated by *The Wives Excuse*.

SMITH, JOHN HARRINGTON. *The Gay Couple in Restoration Comedy*. Cambridge: Harvard Univ. Press, 1948. Significant study including an analysis of *The Wives Excuse* in the context of the 1690s.

STROUP, THOMAS B. "Philosophy and Drama," *Times Literary Supplement*, January 19, 1933, p. 40. Note connecting a passage in *The Loyal Brother* to Dryden, Howard, and Descartes.

SUMMERS, MONTAGUE. "The Source of Southerne's *The Fatal Marriage*," *Modern Language Review* 11(April 1916): 149 - 55. Corrects Hamelius and identifies Behn's *History of the Nun, or, The Fair Vow-Breaker* as the source of the tragic plot.

SUTHERLAND, JAMES E. *English Literature of the Late Seventeenth Century*. Oxford: Oxford Univ. Press, 1969. A good survey of the period with particularly sagacious observations on the drama and Southerne's contribution to it.

SWENEY, JOHN R. "The Dedication of Thomas Southerne's *The Wives Excuse* (1692)," *Library* 5th Series, XXV (1970): 154 - 55. Deals with Dryden's dedication and the printing of the quarto.

SYPHER, WYLIE. *Guinea's Captive Kings. British Anti-Slavery Literature of the XVIIIth Century*. Chapel Hill: Univ. of North Carolina Press, 1942. Extended treatment of the "Oroonoko legend" in the "tradition of the noble Negro."

VERNON, P. F. "Marriage of Convenience and the Moral Code of Restoration Comedy," *Essays in Criticism* 12(1962): 370 - 87. Treats the connection between a social reality and Restoration comic conventions.

WILEY, AUTREY NELL, ed. *Rare Prologues and Epilogues*. London: George Allen & Unwin Ltd., 1940. Contains texts and commentary for Dryden's prologues and epilogues to Southerne's plays.

WILSON, JOHN HAROLD. *A Preface to Restoration Drama*. Riverside Studies in Literature. Boston: Houghton Mifflin Company, 1965. A very useful and interesting introductory volume.

Index

149